THE LAST PRIESTHOOD

THE SECRETS OF OUR ENGLISH ALPHABET
(A REVELATION FROM JESUS CHRIST)

WILLIAM E. BEAVERS

WESTBOW
P R E S S
A DIVISION OF THOMAS NELSON

Scripture taken from the New King James Version. Copyright 1979, 1980, 1982 by Thomas Nelson, Inc. Used by permission. All rights reserved Partial definitions taken from the American Heritage Dictionary The "Double Letter Syndrome" and "Alphatology" are trademarks of "The Last Priesthood"

WestBow Press books may be ordered through booksellers or by contacting:

WestBow Press
A Division of Thomas Nelson
1663 Liberty Drive
Bloomington, IN 47403
www.westbowpress.com
1-(866) 928-1240

Because of the dynamic nature of the Internet, any web addresses or links contained in this book may have changed since publication and may no longer be valid. The views expressed in this work are solely those of the author and do not necessarily reflect the views of the publisher, and the publisher hereby disclaims any responsibility for them.

Any people depicted in stock imagery provided by Thinkstock are models, and such images are being used for illustrative purposes only.

Certain stock imagery © Thinkstock.

ISBN: 978-1-4497-1226-6 (sc)
ISBN: 978-1-4497-1227-3 (dj)
ISBN: 978-1-4497-1225-9 (e)

Library of Congress Control Number: 2011921979

Printed in the United States of America

WestBow Press rev. date: 03/14/2011

****

**But I make known to you, brethren,
that the gospel which was preached by me is not according to man.
For I neither received it from man nor was I taught *it*,
but *it came* through the revelation of Jesus Christ.**

GALATIANS 1:11-12

A Message from Above...

I Pray Today for Matthew, Mark, Luke, and John,
David and Daniel, Peter and Paul,
All your Apostles your Disciples, your Prophets,
And Especially I pray for our Lord and Savior Jesus Christ.
For Yours is the Kingdom, Power and Glory forever.
Amen

I give prayer and thanks to all those that put up with my unalienable
ramblings, undeniable faith, and time consuming beliefs...
Without your sacrifices, none of this would have been possible.
To my Son for his ear when my tongue lashed out.
And to my Daughter who sacrificed so much!
To the rest of my family and friends
Who never gave up belief in me,
And to the Lord God for His Merciful Patience And His Almighty Wisdom.

Believe what you choose to believe, discredit what you need to,
For myself the mysterious powers of our Lord God have given
Me the inspiration to write this book!

Awakening early one morning with coffee in hand
I stepped outside to view this land
Wait till I tell you what he showed to me
In the sky so blue it resembled the sea
In clouds as white as the dove
A sign from the Lord above
A great ship from the past
How long would this image last?
From the top it did start to fade
A wisp of smoke from the bottom it now made
The wisp of smoke began to form
The figure of a great man standing in the storm
The lightning rod I did not see
But the staff of life' could it be!

****

"Therefore listen to me, you men of understanding:
Far be it from God *to do* wickedness,
And *from* the Almighty to commit iniquity.

JOB 34:10

****

lest I seem to terrify you by letters.

"For *his* letters," they say, "*are* weighty and
powerful, but *his* bodily presence is weak,
and *his* speech contemptible."

Let such a person consider this,
that what we are in word by letters when we are absent,
such *we will* be in deed when we are present.

2 CORINTHIANS 10:9-11

Two Thousand Ten and Beyond...

Contents

INTRODUCTION

**Are You Ready to learn the ABC's in a way in
which you have never been taught?**

*It is my intention, without prejudice and with a limited understanding of our world,
The balance of good and evil and the part we as humankind play;
To guide you through the mysterious powers of our alphabet.*

Has our Creator given Me the wisdom to fully Understand His Magnificent ways?

*There is little doubt He is still teaching...
At the same time I do feel comfortable in being able to share with you
That which He has given to us all.*

*As we get started;
You must first realize that the proof is in the letters and words of our
Vocabulary themselves.*

*It will be up to you alone to choose to Accept or Deny
That which we are about to Explore.*

*As we go through each letter of the Alphabet I will do my best to clarify their
True Significance for us All:*

*How Can the Alphabetic letters play a part in our
Destiny, Our Worlds, in your life?
The Answer is simple; we are given, "God Given Names"!*

*The "Names" instilled upon us at Birth were
Ultimately given to us by our LORD God.*

*There are several purposes for each Alphabetic letter.
As we continue to go through all twenty-six letters
remember it might just be possible
That certain things will pertain more to you than to another.*

*As Mankind has progressed through life,
Have the letters and language?
Or Might it be the other way around?*

**Our Alphabet Has Evolved through the
Hebrew, Greek, And Roman Times!**

It is my wish that once you fully understand the mysteries of the "Alphabet"
You too will find belief as I have...

Jesus was a "Common" Man, Keep this in mind as we begin...

Each letter has a "true" Definition,
A definition that explains all those "Common"
words that begin with that same letter...
(Finding time for more complicated words is difficult)

Each letter will also give to us our own Individual Rewards and Punishments;
Each according to the Names we were given,
And the faith and belief we carry within Ourselves!

The More "Belief", The More the Rewards...
Sinning leads to the Punishments...

He does not expect us to be perfect; He is just looking for us to make an effort.
Our Lord God understands Evil is very powerful
and that we tend to stray occasionally.

Acknowledgment Is What He Wants!

We constantly ask ourselves if there is a God,
Why is He so Cruel or where is He when we need Him?

I do not pretend to have all the answers,
But maybe I can give you a few things to think about.

Our Lord God needs our faith to be strong; Our faith needs to be tested...

By taking away our loved ones,
By giving us financial hardships or by simply tempting us;
He is working to build our faith, to build our Character,
To strengthen our very Souls...

Where is He when We need Him?

Realize millions of us are out there that want or need Him but most importantly;
You must also realize that evil does exist and that maybe, just maybe,
Our Lord God is in a constant battle with Satan.

How time consuming that must be!

It is my belief that through faith He will come to us in our most trying times.

(I do feel comfortable in saying this, because I have had that ultimate experience).

But that is another story...

What we must learn is that there are reasons why He works the way He does;
And that no matter what happens to us in this world,
He is preparing us for another.

As we begin to explore the mysteries of the Alphabet farther,
Remember to keep in mind the initials and/or other Capitol letters
Which belong to you.

You may also want to remember those letters that are missing from
"Your life path"

These letters Will Require you to work harder to obtain their Secrets...

Is food considered a Reward?
Will you be able to Understand?

The most Important Aspect of the letters however
is the Message that comes with them!
Try reading through the Entire book before making judgment!
And Remember, it does become quite interesting once we reach the letter "L"?

It is a complicated system otherwise we would
have figured it out on our own.
A "Revelation" is a very powerful experience.
I hope to teach some of it here-within.

****

"Son of man, prophesy and say,
"Thus says the Lord God:

"Wail, 'Woe to the day!'
For the day *is* near,
Even the day of the LORD *is* near;
It will be a day of clouds,
the time of the Gentiles,

EZEKIEL 30:2-3

You can check out the Words in our Dictionary for yourself or with a loved one;
Go through the Experience for Yourself!

Commonality, Rewards and Punishments is where each and every "Common"
Word in our language will fall.
(Some words might tend to fall into several categories)

I have enjoyed the gift I have been given.
My wish is to share it with those that want to learn.

***

Grace to you and peace from Him who is
and who was and who is to come,
and from the seven Spirits who are before His throne,

REVELATION 1:4

Have FUN as you learn about yourself.
Life IS short for most?

As we get closer and closer to those dates in
time that include multiple "T's",
We Will See More Clearly the Rewards and Punishments!

*F*ind out what He truly expects from us....

*E*ach of our letters are Important...

*A*ll of us Are truly wanted...

*R*ead carefully...

Each of us play a part in the struggle between "Good" and "Evil"

Who will you fight for?

***

For behold,
He who forms mountains,
And creates the wind,
Who declares to man what his thought *is*,
And makes the morning darkness,
Who treads the high places of the earth-
The LORD God of hosts *is* His name.

AMOS 4:13

THE ALMIGHTY "A"

ANGELS

A

New, First, Beginning, Start of...

ATTITUDE

ANGER   ALONE

*Ask yourself if the letter "A" looks somewhat similar to the "Mountains",
The "Pyramids" or might it even resemble the "Tepees"?*

All that our Lord God is looking for is "Acknowledgment" and "Acceptance"!

Any one of us?

*Are we looking for the "Answers", they begin by
learning more about our "Alphabet"!*

Another life is where it will lead...

*As we begin to come to a more Thorough Knowledge of the
Power of our Lord God, Realize that the "Alphabet", "starts"
with the letter "A", and ends with the letter "T"!*

Assume the worst...

Amplify...

AMERICA
(Begins and ends with the letter "A")

****

**Therefore thus says the Lord God:
"An adversary *shall* be all around the land;
He shall sap your strength from you,
And your palaces shall be plundered".**

AMOS 3:11-12

*Do You Know the Seven Churches?
We Are the Sixth; "X" Marks the Spot...*

COMMONALITY OF THE LETTER "A"

New Beginnings, Fresh Starts, Being the First.

Each word in our English language shows us this,
Or it falls into a Reward or Punishment.

Bear with me as we examine the commonality of the letter "A":
It does read somewhat like the Dictionary;
My intent is to show you how many of our "Common" words
beginning with the letter "A" fall into this definition...

Aaron: The "original" high priest; older brother of Moses.
Abraham: The "first" patriarch.
Absolute: Unrelated to and independent of anything else.
Acceptance: The act or "first" process of accepting.
Access: You "first" have access to; a means of approaching.
Accident: A "new" and unexpected event or mishap.
Accomplish: To "first" succeed in doing.
Accost: To approach and speak to "first".
Achieve: To "first" accomplish, do or finish with success.
Acid: Used as a "starting" process for making steel.

Acknowledge: To "first" recognize the rights, authority or status of.

Acquire: To come to have as a "new" or added characteristic, trait, or ability.
Action: We must "start" the action before anything is done.
Activate: To "first" set in motion; make active, to "create".
Actor: The "first" to play a part.
Adam: The "first" man.
Adapt: To make fit, as for a specific or "new" use or situation.
Add: To "create" or constitute an addition.
Argument: To "first", bring forward for consideration.
Adjust: To adapt or conform, as to "new" conditions.
Admit: To "first" grant as true or valid.

Adolescence:
The "first" period of physical and psychological development,
From the onset of puberty to maturity.

Adopt: To select and bring into a "new" relationship.
Adult: One who has "first" attained maturity or legal age.

3

Advanced:
"Ahead" of contemporary thought or practices.
(Sounds like Him here)

Advent:
The Coming or "arrival", especially of something Awaited;
The "Re-Birth" of Christ.

Adventure: Disposed to seek adventure or to cope with the "new" and unknown.
Advertise: To make something "first" known, as to advertise a "new" product.
Advice: Acquiring advice can lead to a "new" outlook a "new beginning".
Again: Once more; another time; "anew".
Age: The part of existence extending from the "beginning" to any given time.

Agree: We must "first" agree before we can move on...
Agree: To come into, or be in accord.

Air: Do we not "first" need air when we arrive in this world.
Airplane: Our "first" modern mode of transportation through the skies.
Alert: The "first" period of time during which such a warning is in effect.
Alien: "First" belonging to another country or government.
Alive: "First" having life, in a living state, now living.
Allergy: Altered bodily reactivity to an antigen in response to a "first" exposure.
Allocate: To "first" designate for a special purpose.
Allow: To "first" let do or happen. To acknowledge, or admit.
Ally: To connect or "start" a relationship with.

Alter:
To change or make different, as was "first" considered.
How will we be altered?

Alternative:
A situation presenting a "new" choice or possibility.

"Analyze" This...

Ancestor: Any person from which one is "first" descended.
Ancient: "First" existing, or occurring in times long past.
Another: Different or distinct from the one "first" considered.
Antique: Existing or belonging to "beginnings" or earlier times.

Apostle:
One, who "initiates" a great moral reform or who "first",
Advocates an important belief or system.
The "first" Prominent Christian Missionary to a Region or Group.

We must first make an "Appointment"
We must first "Appreciate" the complexity of it...
We must first get "Approval"
We must first fill out an "Application"
We must first "Appeal" to have our case taken to a higher court...

Approach: The "first" step.
Have you taken the first step yet?

Archeology: Indicates ancient or early times, "beginnings"
Architect: One who "first" designs buildings or advises.

Armageddon: The "beginning" of the final battle between good and evil.

Arrange: To "first" put into a specific order or relation.
Arrive: To "first" reach a destination or particular place.
Art: The "first" real works of its kind.
Artist: One who "creates" works of art.
Ask: To "first" put a question to, to "first" request of or for.
Assign: To "first" set apart for a particular reason.
Astronaut: The "first" man to travel into space.

Atom: One of the minute indivisible particles of which
supposedly is part of the "beginnings" of the universe.

Attack: To "begin" to affect or to act injuriously;
the "beginning" of destructive action.

Attempt: Stresses the initiation or "beginning" of an effort.

Audition: You must "first" pass the audition...
Author: One who "originates" or gives existence to.
Automobile: Our "first" modern mode of transportation...

Even the word "Award" plays a part here, are we
not given an award for "first place"?

How many other "A" words will you find?

5

REWARDS OF THE LETTER "A"

Those things He Rewards or gives to us if we Acknowledge Him and Refrain from Sinning includes "A" words such as:

He gives us the "Ability" to live life...

He Is...
Above: In heaven, heavenward.
Absolute: Perfect in quality or nature; complete.

Absolve: To pronounce clear of blame.
Abstain: To refrain from, to hold back from.
Acceptance: Favorable reception, approval.
Acknowledgment: Recognition of existence.
Active: Capable of functioning, contributing, and participating.
Admirable: Deserving admiration; excellent.
Affection: A fond or tender feeling toward another.
Agile: Able to move in a quick and easy manner.
Agreeable: Pleasing, pleasant to one's liking.
Alert: Vigilantly attentive, watchful.

He "Allows" Us...

Alluring: The power to entice, or tempt.
Always: On every occasion, continuously, forever.
Ambition: A strong desire to achieve, to succeed.

Angel: A spiritual being attendant upon God.

He gives us the "Answers" to our prayers, those that we "truly" need...

Anticipation: To look forward to.
Apology: Expressing regret or asking pardon for a fault.
Appetite: A strong wish or urge to partake of something.
Appreciation: Gratefulness, gratitude.
Articulate: Endowed with the power of speech.

Astonishment: To fill with sudden wonder or amazement.

Atonement:
Amends for an injury or wrong;
The Reconciliation of God and Man.

Attention: Observant consideration, notice.
Attraction: The quality of attracting, allure, and charm.
Awake: To stir the interest of, excite.

How "Awesome" is He...

****

"Therefore whoever hears these sayings of Mine,
and does them,
I will liken him to a wise man who built his house on the rock;
"and the rain descended,
the floods came,
and the winds blew and beat on that house;
and it did not fall,
for it was founded on the rock.

MATTHEW 7:24-25

****

"Therefore being exalted to the right hand of God,
and having received from the Father the promise of the Holy Spirit,
He poured out this which you now see and hear.

ACTS 2:33

I am a Servant of our Lord and Savior and do-not pretend to be perfect,
I have simply been chosen to fulfill GODS word.
I too am learning as we travel into uncharted waters...

****

But the LORD *is* with me as a mighty, awesome One.

JEREMIAH 20:11

PUNISHMENTS OF THE LETTER "A"

Those things that befall us if we choose to follow the path of Evil Include:

Abandon: To forsake, desert. (We will be tested)

Abnormal: Not normal, deviant.
Abolish: Do away with; put an end to.
Abuse: To use wrongfully or improperly.
Accident: An unexpected and undesirable event.
Alone: Apart from others, solitary, with nothing further.
Amuck: In a blind heedless manner.
Anger: A feeling of extreme displeasure, hostility or indignation.
Angry: Incensed or enraged. **(How Angry is He)?**
Anxiety: A state of uneasiness and distress, worry.

Argument: A quarrel, contention, a reason of matter for dispute.
Ashamed: Feeling shame or guilt.

Ass: A vain, self important, silly or stupid person.
Awful: Extremely bad or unpleasant.
Awkward: Not graceful, ungainly.

*Are there few punishments because the "A" representing a learning experience
Allows us a little reprieve?*

*There are other words that will fit into both categories,
Spend some time by yourself or with your loved ones and see what the
Lord God gives us with the capitol letter "A".*

*Might it be possible that for each and every time
we allow ourselves to be tempted,
Or we just out and out break one of His laws
we receive a punishment of sorts?*

*Might it be possible that each time we do good;
each day that passes without sin,
We receive some sort of reward?*

Try to keep this in mind as we explore the mysteries of our Alphabet...

*When things become tough for us, Might this
just be a "test" from our Lord God?*

*Refrain from becoming "Angry", lose the bad
"Attitude" and see what happens...*

"Ask" and you shall receive...

*Surely there is more to the "A" letter than just mere Coincidence?
Our Lord God works in mysterious ways.*

*Can the Alphabet play a significant part in our
lives, for me the "Answer" is clear.*

*Breakdown any word that starts with the letter "A";
In this instance I will use the word "Apostle"*

*The letter "A" = first of; one that begins something new; the definition seems to fit.
The letter "P" = A more "profound purpose": fits the word...
The letter "O" = Serves purpose for "Others", completes the cycle of; fits here also.
The letter "S" = The "traveler"; seems like it would fit...
The letter "T" = "Tribulation, Test, etc.; fits (read about the twelve in the bible)
The letter "L"= "Life made easier after getting through the tough start.
The letter "E" = An "Earthly figure", Effects Everywhere; Everyone; Everything.*

Seems we get a pretty clear definition of this word!

*All those Words fitting under the definition of "Commonality"
can be done in the same Way using the Twenty-Six
Set definitions given by our Lord and Savior!*

****

**But this I confess to you,
that according to the Way which they call a sect,
so I worship the God of my fathers,
believing all things which are written
in the Law and in the Prophets.**

ACTS 24:14

Notes

ALL ABOUT THE LETTER "A"

The "A" is "Awesome", it includes "All" things!

*Are you "Aware" that you might work as an
"Anthropologist" or an "Architect"?
Might you teach "Algebra" or are you an "Actor"?
Could you be an "Attorney" or an "Aeronautical Engineer"?
Might you be a professional "Athlete"?*

*Is "Astrology" part of your life?
Do you own an "Art" store or an "Auto" repair shop?*

*Any way you look at it the "A" will play a part in your life.
Are you "Aware" you could be an "Alcoholic"?
Or that you may be prone to "Allergies"?
Do you have "Asthma"?*

*Do you want "Answers" or are you "Absentminded"?
Do you use those words that begin with the letter "A" often?
Have you ever seen an "Angel" or are you just "Alluring"?
Can you "Accept" things easily, or do you get "Angry"?
Will you demand an "Apology" or will you continue to "Argue"?*

"Acknowledgment" in our Lord God is the Key!

*You Are the "first" to try new things...
The Capitol letter "A" represents **"new beginnings"**,
Might you tend to "start" things over and over again?*

*The letter "A" gives us the "Ability" to do many **"new"** things.
Might it give us such "Abilities", as staying
"Awake" for longer periods of time?
There is still much to be uncovered in "The Power of our Alphabet"*

"Are" you prepared to "Answer" to Him?

*Give to more than those that are Hungry...
"Atonement"*

Rest "Assured" our Lord God is "Available"

He Does Know When We Are Not Sincere!

11

**

As I worked on the Computer late one Night'
Behold an Awesome Sight!
Five signs from above...
The Dinosaur was the first of these,
Then the sign of Man with which He was well pleased.
The Towers were next as We have seen...
Soon came man redeemed' "a tiny cross then gleamed"!
Pyramids' As slick as glass is what I saw next,
And Mountains of it,
Is this where the "Thousand Year Reign" did sit?

****

And it shall come to pass in the last days, says God'
That I will pour out My Spirit on all flesh;
Your sons and your daughters shall prophesy,
Your young men shall see visions,
Your old men shall dream dreams.
And on My menservants and on My maidservants
I will pour out My Spirit in those days;
And they shall prophesy.
I will show wonders in heaven above
And signs in the earth beneath;
Blood and fire and vapor of smoke.
The sun shall be turned into darkness,
And the moon into blood,
Before the coming of the great and
awesome day of the LORD.
And it shall come to pass
That whoever calls on the name of the LORD Shall be saved.

ACTS 2:17-21

Notes

BEHOLD THE "B"

BELIEF

The "Birth" and the "Blood" of Jesus Christ!

B

Turned sideways it resembles a pair of glasses,
this is the first clue into this letter...

Watched more closely, seen more clearly...

BLASPHEMY

Beware, He sees all...

Because you have the letter "B" in your name
Might "Belief" come a little easier for you than those without it?

Belief is what will make life less of a struggle...

Be prepared...

Blasphemy will lead us to His punishments...
(Thou shall not use thy Lords name in vain; refrain from damning God)

Begin your day with a prayer...

By setting a "Better" example might we make our
Children's lives a little less difficult?
(He does punish not only us, but our future generations as well)

****

The fear of the LORD *is* the beginning of knowledge,
***But* fools despise wisdom and instruction.**

PROVERBS 1:7

Best to Be ready...
Breaking your old habits will be tough...
Brace yourself as we examine all those things in "this" world that our
Lord God is "watching" a little closer.

Bet on it...

****

"I am the Alpha and the Omega, the Beginning and the End,"
says the Lord,
"who is and who was and who is to come, the Almighty."

REVELATION 1:8

16

COMMONALITY OF THE LETTER "B"

Watched More Closely, Seen More Clearly!

The "B" gives us a fresh outlook;

Does our Lord God "See" those with the letter "B" more Clearly?

Decide for yourself;
The following are a list of some of our most common "B" words:

From "Baal" to the "Byway" He "Sees" the "B"!

**

He sees the "Babies" and He sees the "Baboon"

He sees the "Bachelor" and He sees behind your "Back"

He sees your "Backbone" and He sees the "Back-door"

He sees the "Background" the "Backhand" and the "Backseat"

He sees "Backstage" and the "Backstop"

He sees us when we "Back-talk", and when we go "Backwards"

He sees us when we "Backup" and when we "Backtrack"

He sees us when we are in the "Backyard"

He sees the "Bacon", The "Beans" and the "Bacteria"

He sees us when we act "Bad"

He sees us when we are "Baffled"

He is watching us when we "Bake"

He is watching from the "Balcony"

He sees the "Bagel" and the "Baggage" we carry...

What about the "Bald eagle", and when we go "Bald"

He sees us when we are out playing "Ball"

He sees the "Banana" and He is watching the "Band"

He sees when we need a "Bandage" or a "Band-Aid"

He sees our "Bankroll" and when we go "Bankrupt"

He sees the "Banner" and especially the "Banquet"

For sure He is watching the "Baptism"

He sees us when we act "Barbaric", and when we throw a "Barbecue"

He sees the "Barber", and when our cabinets are "Bare"

He even sees a "Bargain"

He is watching the "Barley" grow...

He sees the "Barn" and the "Barracks"

He sees things that are "Barren" and when we set up a "Barricade"

He sees the "Barriers" we set before ourselves...

He is watching the "Bartender"

He might even be out watching the "Basketball" game...

He sees the "Bass" and the "Basset hound"

He sees us when we take a "Bath" and when the "Battery" goes dead...

He Sees All Our "Battles"

Might He be out watching the "Bay"?

He sees the "Beachcomber", and He sees the "Beacon"

He sees the "Beads" and the "Beagle"

He sees the "Beam" of light and He sees the "Bear"

He is watching when we grow a "Beard" and when we take a "Beating"

Surely He sees all the "Beauty"!

He is watching the "Beaver", and just "Because"

How about the "Bee"?

Is He checking on the "Beetle"?

He sees us when we "Beg", and He saw the "Beginning"!

He sees our "Behavior" and our "Belief"!

He sees us when we "Bellow"; and He sees our "Bellies"

He sees when we "Belong"

He is watching when we use the "Belt"

Can He See "Beneath"?

Can He See what is "Beneficial" for us?
Rest assured in your faith...

He sees us when we are at our "Best"

He sees us when we make a "Bet"

He sees us when we "Betray" someone and when we try to do "Better"

He sees "Between" the lines...

Can our Lord God see "Beyond"?

Might He be watching us when we read the "Bible"!
(Two B's in the word Bible)

He sees your "Bewilderment"!

"Believe"

I have seen His image on numerous occasions...

That is a lot of B's but wait there are many more!

He sees us when we learn to ride the "Bicycle," and when we grow "Big"

He sees the "Big brother" and the "Big-mouth"

He sees the "Bigot" and He sees "Big-time"

He sees when the "Bill's" pile up...

He even sees the "Billboard"

Might He see a "Billion" things at once?

He sees us when we get in a "Bind"

He sees us through "Binoculars"!

He is watching our "Biological clock", He sees the "Biopsy"

He has a "Bird's-eye" view!

He is watching on your "Birthday", surely He saw your "Birth"!

He sees the "Bishop"

He is watching the "Bitch"

He sees us when we "Bite" and when we are "Bitter"

He sees when things get "Bizarre"

He sees the "Black-bird" and the little "Black-book"

He sees those that "Blackmail" and the "Black-market"

He sees the "Blade" and He sees "Blame"

He sees the "Black-oak" and the "Black-out"

He sees the "Blank" expression and the "Blanket"

There is no doubt that He sees the "Blasphemy"!

He sees when we are "Blind" and when we are "Blindfolded"

He sees us when we "Blink" and He sees the "Blister"

Find Our Lord God and you too will be able to see the "Bliss"!

Do you believe He saw the "Blood" of Christ?

He sees the flowers "Blooming", and when they "Blossom"

He sees when the wind is "Blowing" and He sees the "Blue" skies...

He is watching the "Bluebird" or might it be the "Bluegill"

He sees the "Blueprint", might He have already made it...

He sees us when we have the "Blues"

He sees us when we try to "Bluff"

He sees when we "Blush"

He sees us when we "Boast", and when we are on a "Boat"

He is watching the "Bobtail" and the "Bobwhite"

He watches us when we "Boil", and when we act "Bold"

He sees the "Bolt" and the "Bomb"

He is watching when we "Bond" with our children...

He sees when we break a "Bone"

He sees when we get a "Bonus" and when we read a "Book"

He sees when we "Borrow"

He is watching the "Boss"

He sees when we "Botch" things up and when we hit the "Bottle"

You Can know for sure that He Can see the "Bottom line"!

He sees when things are "Bountiful"

He sees the "Boutique", and when we "Bow" down...

He is watching when we go "Bowling" and when we open the "Box"

He sees us when we use our "Brains"

He sees when the "Brakes" are bad...

He sees us when we act "Brave"

He sees us when we "Brawl"

He sees us when we eat "Bread" and when we "Break" all the rules...

****

"For the great day of His wrath has come, and who is able to stand?"

REVELATION 6:17

He sees the things that are "Breakable"

He is watching when we have a "Breakdown"

He sees our "Breath" and when we "Breed"

He sees the "Breeze" and the "Bribery" that goes on...

He is checking out the "Bride"

He sees the "Briefest" encounter...

The "Bright" lights are easy for Him to see, as is our "Brilliance"!

He sees when our cup is filled to the "Brim"

He sees when we "Bring" sin into our lives!

He sees the "Broach" and the "Broccoli"

He sees when things are "Brought" to us, and the color "Brown"

He sees when we are "Bruised"

He is watching our "Budget"

How about the "Buffalo"?

He is checking out the "Buffet"

He sees the "Bugs" and the horse-drawn "Buggy"

He sees us when we "Build" our house...

He even sees the light "Bulb"

He sees the "Bullet" and the "Bulletin" that you just posted...

Might He be watching the "Bullfrog" or the "Bullfight"?

Can He see the "Bull's Eye" or just the "Bullshit"?

He is keeping an eye on the "Bully" and the "Bum"

He sees us when we "Bump" into something in the middle of the night,

And when we "Bundle" up...

Surely, He can see our "Burdens"!

He sees all the "Bureaucracy" in this country...

Might He be out watching the "Burglar"?

He sees the trees when they "Burn" and He sees the dam when it "Bursts"

What does He think when He sees the "Butcher"?

You can bet He sees the beauty of the "Butterfly"

He sees when we lose a "Button" and when we "Buy" something new...

He sees when we wave "Bye"

All these "B" words and many, many, more.
Looks to me like our Lord God sees all!
Believe that He is watching us!

Look up how many other things He sees in your favorite Dictionary!
And do not forget the "Bible"

23

****

Beloved,
let us love one another,
for love is of God;
and everyone who loves is born of God and knows God.
He who does not love does not know God, for God is love.
In this the love of God was manifested towards us,
that God has sent His only begotten Son into the world,
that we might live through Him.
In this is love, not that we loved God,
but that He loved us
and sent His Son *to be* the propitiation for our sins.
Beloved, if God so loved us, we also ought love one another.

1 JOHN 4:7-11

Therefore, beloved,
looking forward to these things,
be diligent to be found by Him in peace,
without spot and blameless;
and consider *that* the longsuffering of our Lord *is* salvation -
as also our beloved brother Paul,
according to the wisdom given to him,
has written to you,
as also in all the epistles,
speaking in them of these things,
in which are some things hard to understand,
which untaught and unstable *people* twist to their own destruction,
as *they do* also the rest of the Scriptures.
You therefore, beloved, since you know *this* beforehand,
beware lest you also fall from your own steadfastness,
being led away with the error of the wicked;
but grow in the grace and knowledge of our
Lord and Savior Jesus Christ.
To Him *be* the glory both now and forever.
Amen.

2 PETER 3:14-18

REWARDS OF THE LETTER "B"

What Rewards are given to those that have the Dominate "B"?

A Baby!
Thou shall go forth and multiply...
(Is now the right time)?

Balance: A stable mental or psychological state.
Bargain: Something offered or acquired at an advantageous price.
Basis: The chief or most stable component of anything.
Beauty: A pleasing quality associated with harmony of form.

Belief: The mental act, condition, or habit of placing trust or confidence in
A person or thing; faith.

Belonging: A close and secure relationship.
Best: Surpassing all others in quality; most excellent.
Better: Greater in excellence or higher in quality.

Blessed: Enjoying happiness; fortunate.

Bold: Fearless and daring; courageous.
Bountiful: Abundance and plentiful.
Brain: Used by highly intelligent people.
Bravery: Possessing or displaying courage; valiant.

Breathtaking: Inspiring awe; exciting.
Brilliance: Splendor; Magnificence.

Brotherhood: The quality of being brotherly; fellowship.

There are many other Rewards that also fall
under the commonality of the "B",
How many do you see?

Believe the Lord God Sees All.

Does it make sense that because we live in a world filled with sin...

That He Sees More Evil?

PUNISHMENTS OF THE LETTER "B"

We Can be Punished with the following…

Babble: a confusion of words or sounds.
Bad: Inferior; poor; evil; wicked; sinful.
Baffled: To foil; thwart; frustrate.
Banishment: To force to leave; to drive away.
Barren: Not producing offspring: childless or fruitless.
Barrier: Anything, material or immaterial, that acts to obstruct or prevent passage.

He gives us "Bashful", "Battery" and the "Battle", "Beaten", and a "Beating"

He gives us "Befooled" and the "Beggar"

He gives us "Beguiled" and our bad "Behavior"

He gives us the "Belch" and "Below"

He "Besets" us with problems, He "Be-siege's" us with worry…

He gives us "Betrayal", "Bewildered", "Biased" and all the "Bickering"

He gives us the "Bigot" and the drinking "Binge"

He punishes us with "Bitterness", and the "Blabbermouth"

Could He have even punished us with the "Black Death"?

He puts us on the "Black-list", gives us the "Black-eye" and He gives us "Blame"

He gives us "Blatant" and "Bleak"

Could He be punishing us with the "Blizzard, or just the "Bloodbath"?

Does He punish us by giving us the "Blues" or by causing the "Blunder"?

Might He be punishing us with the "Bogey"?

You can bet the "Bomb" does a lot of punishment…
(Two "B's" in the word bomb)

Might He just give us being "Bored" or plain "Boring"?

If we "Botch" things up is that a form of His punishment?

Could He just give us those things that are "Bothersome"?

Could He be punishing us with the "Brawl" or the "Breach of Promise"?

The "Breakdown" and the "Break-up" could both be forms of punishment...

He punishes us with the "Bruise" the "Brute" and the "Buffoon"

Is the "Bullet" our punishment or just being "Bullish"?

If we "Bungle", an assignment is that His way of dishing out punishment?

Might He just give us all the "Burdens"?

On the other hand:
Might He just make us "Bushed" or to "Busy"
to enjoy the life He has given us?

Belief in our Lord God is what He desires.
Read the Bible, be strong and;

"BELIEVE"

****

I write to you, little children,
Because your sins are forgiven you for His name's sake.
I write to you, fathers,
Because you have known Him *who is* from the beginning.
I write to you, young men,
Because you have overcome the wicked one.
I write to you, little children,
Because you have known the Father.
I have written to you, fathers,
Because you have known Him *who is* from the beginning.
I have written to you, young men,
Because you are strong, and the word of God abides in you,
And you have overcome the wicked one.

1 JOHN 2:12-14

All ABOUT THE LETTER "B"

Are you a "Banker", a "Bartender" or a "Beautician"?
Might you be a "Botanist" or a "Biochemist"?
You could be a "Bachelor" or own a "Bakery"

Might you be a "Border-agent", a "Broadcaster" or a "Biker"?
Maybe you deliver "Babies" or work at the "Ballpark"?

Do you enjoy running around in your "Bare feet"?
Do you know a "Bargain" when you see it?

Do you enjoy "Baseball", "Basketball" or do you like the "Bow and Arrow"?

Are you into "Books", remember the "Bible" has two "B's"

Could the "Bonbon" be your favorite, or just the "Beer"?

Might you just like "Bread" and "Butter"?

Do you work for "Burlington" or "Boeing"?

You can "Bet" the Lord God is watching you a little closer than others...

Do you use those words that begin with the letter "B" often?

The letter "B" is your world, try to refrain from all the "Bragging"

With "True Belief" all things are possible...

Believe in our Lord God, Bet that He has a Plan for You!

****

He who believes in the Son of God has the witness in himself;
he who does not believe God has made Him a liar,
because he has not believed the testimony
that God has given of His Son.

1 JOHN 5:10

CONVICTION IS THE KEY

CHRIST

CHERISHED

Children   Church   Chosen

C

The Capitol letter "C"
Lacks "true" Conviction...
(It can be achieved; Jesus Christ is our example)
"Conviction" is a tough word in itself, notice the two separate letter "C's"
Like it or not the "C" is a tough letter,
However it does give us many forms of Reward!

ALL THE "COMPLAINING"

Conviction is the key that will unlock the door to His world...

Can having the letter "C" in your name give you more "Choices"?

Choosing between "Good and Evil" can be difficult for some...

Cherish the things that you have...
Celebrate...
Children need to be taught...
Consider all the possibilities...

*Challenge those around you through the power of "**His**" letters...*

(The "CH", the "A", the Double "LL", two
"E's", the "N" and the "G";
WOW, what a word...

Changing the way you think will take some "Conviction"
Christ begins with the "Ch", how much can we learn from those letters?

(The "Church" begins and ends with the letters "Ch")
The School, the Scholar, the Teacher, the Preacher, and the "Coach"
Include the "Ch" letters...

*Are you a **Christ**ian?*
*Might you be a **Christ**ina or a **Christ**opher?*

Clearly, He has given us a message through the "Alphabet"!

****

In the law it is written:

"With men of other tongues and other lips I will speak to this people;
And yet, for all that, they will not hear Me"

Says the Lord.

1 CORINTHIANS 14:21

COMMONALITY OF THE LETTER "C"

Conviction and/or the lack of it!

*We tend to struggle with true belief, the letter "C"
is filled with words that express this!*

*"Check" out if you will the following "C" words;
I believe you too will see the similarities as I have that show
us that the "C" fits into the Above definition...*

How much can we count on the following?

Cab: When was the last time you had to wait for one?

Cabin: A "part time" shelter.

Cable television: How reliable is yours?

Can we rely on the "Caddy" or the "Cadet"?

How long does the "Caffeine" keep us going?

Do we always get the "Calcium" we need?

Calculation: An estimate based upon probability.

*Calendar: Any of "various" systems of reckoning time.
(We have numerous calendars in our world, which one is most reliable)?*

*Camera: Do the pictures you take always come
out, or does it always work properly?*

Camp: A "temporary" lodging in tents, huts or other makeshift shelters.

"Can" we always do what we are supposed to do?

Will the "Candle and the "Coal" eventually burn out?

"Canoe", does it not have a tendency to flip over?

How "Capable" Are you, or how reliable is your "Car"?

How often can you count on getting the "Card" you need?

How certain are you that your "Career" will last?

31

Are we always "Careful" or are we sometimes "Careless"?

Will the "Cargo" always arrive?

Is the "Carnival" here today and gone tomorrow?

Does the "Carpet" need to be replaced?

Does the "Carton" always protect the eggs?

Is the "Case" always solved?

Does the "Cashier" always give us the correct change or charge the right price?

Do we always "Catch" the ball?

Do we always use "Caution" when we should?

Will the "Ceiling" fall, or can we rely on the "Cellar" not to flood?

Will the "Cement" crack?

Will the "Cent" be worth as much tomorrow as it is today?

Will there be another "Century"?

Is the "Cereal" always fresh?

Chafe: to wear away, or irritate by rubbing.

How reliable is the "Chain"? (I have broken more than a few)

When was the last time you broke a "Chair"? (Or fell from one)

Can you stand up to the "Challenge"?

Are you willing to take a "Chance"?

Chance: The abstract nature of quality shared by unexpected, random, or "unpredictable" events!

Change: The word speaks for itself...

Is "Chaos" predictable?

****

**I do not write these things to shame you,
but as my beloved children I warn *you*.**

1 CORINTHIANS 4:14

Chapter: A period or sequence of events that marks a distinct "change" of pattern.

Char: To reduce to charcoal by "incomplete" combustion.

Are you always in "Charge"?

Can we count on the "Charity"?

Will your "Charm" always work?

Chasm: a sudden interruption of continuity.

Are things always "Cheap", or do we sometimes "Cheat"?

Does the "Check" always clear the bank?

Is the "Cheese" always fresh or does it sometimes get moldy?

How reliable are the "Chemicals"?

Does the "Cherry Tree" always produce fruit?

Can we rely on the "Child"?

Do you sometimes feel "Chilly"?

Is "Chivalry" still with us or is it dead?

*"Choice" is a very big word.
(How often do we stick to the choices we have made)?*

Choose wisely and all things can be yours!

Do you always get your "Chores" done?

*Does the "Church" lack true conviction?
(Do they all teach the same things)?*

Will the "Cinema" always show your favorite movie?

Circuit: A closed, "usually" circular curve.

How is your conviction when it comes to keeping things "Clean"?

Are things always "Clear" for you?

Do we sometimes "Cling" to the past?

Does the "Clock" always tell the correct time?

**When was the last time you watched the
"Clouds", do they not come and go?**
*(Spend some time watching them you might be amazed at what you see,
And remember in the latter days even Satan can control them.)*

Does the "Coast line" always remain the same?

Eventually the "Code" will be broken…

Will the "Coin" be worth the same?

Does the "Cold" not come and go?

Is the "Color" always clear?

Is the "Column" always printed?

Do you always "Comb" your hair?

Does the "Comet" come and go?

How reliable is your "Commute"?

Do we always "Communicate when we should?

Are we always fairly "Compensated"?

Are things always "Completed" when they need to be?

Are things always "Complex", or do we sometimes "Compromise"?

*Some of us know how unreliable the "Computer" can be…
(It is a wonderful tool however)*

Do we always "Concentrate"?

Surely, you are not always "Conceded"?

Do we always make "Concessions"?

When was the last time they canceled your favorite "Concert"?

How reliable is the "Condom"?

Is your "Conduct" always proper, or do you always "Confess"?

Is your "Confidence" always with you or does it sometimes lack?

Do the "Conflicts" come and go?

Are you always "Confused"?

Do we always "Congratulate" those that deserve it?

Is the "Connection" always strong?

Do we always "Consider" both sides?

Do you sometimes forget to wear your "Contacts"?

Are you always in "Contention"?

Is the "Contract" reliable?

Do we always "Contribute" to the needy?

Are you always in "Control"?

Convert: to "change" into another form, substance, state, or product.

Does the "Convertible" top always work, or keep the rain out?

Do we always "Convey" the message?

Are you always "Convinced"?

Do you always "Cooperate"?

"How reliable is the "Cop"?
(Where are they when you need one)?

35

Are you always "Correct"?

Do we always find the "Courage"?

Do we always "Cram" for the test?

Craze: A "short" lived popular fashion, a rage; fad.

Do we always get the "Credit" we deserve?

How reliable is your "Crew"?

Is the "Crime" always the same?

Are you always a "Critic"?

Does the "Crop" always flourish?

Do we always "Cross" at the intersection?

Are you always "Cruel"?

Do we sometimes go on a "Crusade"?

Do we always "Crush" the opponent?

Do you always "Cuddle"?

Do we always find the "Culprit"?

Will the "Culture" remain the same?

Do you always see the "Curve" ahead?

Are you always home by "Curfew"?

Might you sometimes get a little "Curious"?

We know how unreliable the "Current" and the "Currency" are!

Again, there are many, many, more "C" words...

"Check" out the Dictionary for yourself!

Let us not forget the "Cell Phone"

Our lack of "Conviction" stands out in the Eye's of our Lord God.

"Can" He forgive us?

****

if indeed you continue in the faith, grounded and steadfast,
and are not moved away from the hope of the gospel
which you heard, which was preached to every creature
under heaven, of which I, Paul, became a minister.

COLOSSIANS 1:23

And whatever you do in word or deed,
do all in the name of the Lord Jesus,
giving thanks to God the Father through Him.

COLOSSIANS 3:17

Remember the More we believe the more "Conviction" we receive!

How much different is it to have the "CH" instead of just the "C"?

There is much still left to discover!

I did not choose but was chosen...

REWARDS OF THE LETTER "C"

Calculated: Estimated with forethought.
Calm: Not excited or agitated.
Can: Ability; possession of a specific right or means.
Candid: Without prejudice; impartial; fair.

Might He give us the "Candy"?

Candor: Frankness of expression; Sincerity; straightforwardness.
Canny: Having or showing knowledge and skill, fully competent.
Capability: Competent; Efficient: Able.
Capacity: The ability to receive, hold or absorb.
Captivation: To fascinate by special charm or beauty.

He Does "Care"!

Carefree: Free of worries and responsibilities.
Careful: Cautious in though, speech or action; prudent.
Caress: a gentle touch or gesture of fondness, tenderness, or love.
Cause: Good or sufficient reason or ground.
Celebration: Celebrate our Lord God!
Certainty: The fact, quality, or state of being certain.
Champion: One who fights for, defends, or supports a cause.

Does He give us a "Chance"?

Character: A description of ones Attributes, traits or abilities.
Charm: The power or quality of pleasing, attracting, or fascinating.
Cheerful: Being in good spirits; happy, pleasant.
Cherish: to hold dear; treat with affection and tenderness.

He gives us "Children"!

Chivalry: Qualities such as bravery, courtesy and honesty.

Because of the sacrifice of Jesus Christ we get;

Choice:
That which is best or preferable above others.

Did He not give us "Christ"!

Civilized: Polite or cultured.
Clear: Free from anything that dims, obscures or darkens.
Clever: Mentally quick and original.

Does He give us "Closure"?

As we continue with the "C" words that represent our rewards,
Remember that we are given many choices...
Therefore, it makes sense that we are also given many rewards.

Co-existence: The condition of living together.
Cognizance: Conscious knowledge or recognition.
Comfort: A state of ease or well-being.

Are we Rewarded if we follow the "Commandments"?

Commitment: A giving in charge or entrusting.
Communication: The art and technology of communicating.
Compassion: The deep feeling of sharing the suffering of another.

Compatible: Capable of living or performing in harmonious,
Agreeable or congenial combination with others.

Competent: Properly or well qualified; capable.
Complete: Having all necessary or normal parts; entire; whole.
Composed: Calm; serene; self-possessed.

Is one of our Rewards being able to "Compromise"?

Are "Condolences" a form of reward?

Are we rewarded with good "Conduct"?

Are we rewarded when we "Confess"?

Are we rewarded with the ability to "Conquer" our fears?

Is the "Consummation" a reward for when we marry?

Might He just reward us with being "Content"?

Will He Reward us if we show true "Conviction"?
(Of course He will)

If we can "Convince" others, will we then be rewarded?

Are we rewarded when we "Cooperate"?

Is being able to "Cope" with the situation our reward?

Might the "Copyright" be a reward or does it lack "conviction"?

Cornucopia:
A goat's horn overflowing with fruit, flowers and corn, signifying prosperity.

Is being "Correct" our reward?

Coupon: A detachable part of a ticket, advertisement, or other certificate entitling the bearer to certain stated benefits such as a cash refund or a gift.

Courage:
The state or quality of mind or spirit that enables us to face danger with self-possession, Confidence, and Resolution.

Does He reward us with "Courtesy"?

Is just being "Cozy" our reward?

Is the ability to "Create" a way in which we are rewarded?

Are we rewarded with good "Credit"?

Is the "Crucifix" the Lord Gods way of reminding us of the rewards He gave to us by sacrificing his son?

Are we rewarded with the vacation "Cruise"?

Does He reward us with the "Cure"?

Might He just give us that "Cushy" job?

Does He reward us "Custody" of our children?

Might He give us the "Custom" built home?

Is being "Cute" a reward?

There are many ways in which our Lord God can reward us!
The letter "C" gives Him many choices.

PUNISHMENTS OF THE LETTER "C"

As with the Rewards, the Punishments can also be numerous:

Cadaver: a dead body, especially one intended for dissection.

Is being "Callous" a form of punishment?

Could "Cancer" be a form of punishment or even the "Canker" sore?

Is being held "Captive" a punishment?

Is "Cardiac" Arrest our punishment?

Is being "Careless"?

Carnage: Massive slaughter, as in war; massacre.

Carouse: Boisterous, drunken.

How about the "Casket", "Castaway" or "Castrated"?

Is being a "Casualty" a form of punishment?

How about the "Catapult" or the "Catastrophe"?

Is the "Cavity" a punishment?

What about the word "Cemetery"?

Is "Chaos" a form of punishment or how about the "Charley" horse?

Chasten: To "punish", either physically or morally; chastise.

If we have to listen to the "Chatterbox" or deal with the "Cheat",

Are those ways that our Lord God punishes us?

Chide: To scold; rebuke; reprimand, to state ones disapproval of.

Is being "Childish" "Chilly" or "Chintzy" forms of punishment?

If we "Choke" or have high "Cholesterol" is that our punishment?

For sure the "Chores" are a form of punishment!

Are we punished with the "Citation"?

41

Is the "Clap" our punishment for being promiscuous?

How about the "Close Call", the Blood "Clot", or the "Clutter"?

Is the "Cock-roach" a form of punishment?

The "Coffin" starts with the letter "C" as does getting the "Cold Shoulder"?

Does the "Collision" represent punishment or how about the "Coma"?

We all know how punishing the "Commute" can be!

Is "Complaint" or being "Complicated" forms of punishment?
Is "Compulsive", "Conceited", or the "Concussion" punishments?
Is "Condescending", "Confinement", or the "Conflict" our punishments?

Are you "Confused" or just "Congested"?

Are we not required to face the "Consequences" for our actions?

Are "Constraint", "Contagious", "Contaminated", "Contempt",
"Contraband" "Contradiction" and "Contrite", all forms of His punishments?

Am I stirring up a "Controversy"?

Is the "Convict" serving his punishment?

Is the "Convulsion" or the "Coronary" forms of punishment?

Is the "Corpse" or being "Corruptible" forms of punishment?

Are we prepared to pay the "Cost" for our sins,
or will we simply ask for forgiveness?

****

Behold, I tell you a mystery:
We shall not all sleep, but we shall all be changed - in a moment,
in the twinkling of an eye, at the last trumpet.
For the trumpet will sound, and the dead
will be raised incorruptible,
and we shall be changed.

1 CORINTHIANS 15:52

Is the rising "Cost of living" a way of punishing us?

Might it be the "Court" that will give us our punishment?
The "Court Martial" and the "Court of Appeals" both deal with punishment...

How about the "Cramp" or the "Crap" we put up?

Are the "Cravings" we have, or just going "Crazy" ways to punish us?

*Is the "Creak" in the floor or the "Creature" in
our dreams His way of dealing with us?*

Might we just have to deal with the "Creep"?

Are we punished when we commit a "Crime"?

Having to go through the "Crisis" sounds punishing...

Is dealing with the "Criticism" or the "Crook" punishments?

Being caught in a "Crossfire" or being hit in the "Crotch" seem punishing...

Is being "Crude", "Cruel" or "Crummy" ways to punish us?

Might He just "Crush" us!

Do we "Cry" when things go wrong?

Will the "Culprit" be punished?

The teenager believes the "Curfew" is a punishment...

Is the "Curse" our punishment or is it just being "Cussed" at?

If we are "Cut" or if a "Cyclone" hits are these, our punishments?

CHRIST WAS CRUCIFIED FOR OUR SINS!

****

**If then you were raised with Christ,
seek those things which are above,
where Christ is,
sitting at the right hand of God.**

COLOSSIANS 3:1

ALL ABOUT THE LETTER "C"

Are you a "Carpenter" a "Cosmetologist" or a "Camp Counselor"?
You could be a "Cook" or own a "Coffee" shop...
Might you be the local "Comedian"?

"Children" might play a part in your life...
Do you work for the "City"?
Do you enjoy "Camping"?

Do you enjoy the "Corn", the "Cantaloupe", or the "Cucumbers"?
Do you enjoy "Cereal" in the morning or anytime?
I bet you enjoy having the "Cash"!
The "Circus" is always fun...
Write a "Cookbook" or "Call" up a friend...

"Curiosity" killed the cat...
Choose wisely in all that you do...
The "C" gives you many, many "Choices"

Because you have the letter "C"
Will you tend to take more chances, or might you just get a few extra?
And remember you are cousins to the "K", "Q", and the "S"...

Stick to what you believe in, "Conviction" is the key for you...

The Lord God made A "Choice" for Us!

****

I now rejoice in my sufferings for you,
and fill up in my flesh what is lacking in the afflictions of Christ,
for the sake of His body,
which is the church,
of which I became a minister according the stewardship from God
which was given to me for you,
to fulfill the word of God,
the mystery which has been hidden from ages and from generations,
but now has been revealed to His saints.
To them God willed to make known what are the riches of the glory of this
mystery among the Gentiles: which is Christ in you, the hope of glory.
Him we preach, warning every man and teaching every man in all wisdom,
that we may present every man perfect in Christ Jesus.
To this *end* I also labor,
striving according to His working which works in me mightily.

COLOSSIANS 1:24-29

A THIRD "D" IN DEDICATED

DESTINY

DAD   DAUGHTER   DOG

D

The Capitol Letter "D"
Strength in the "D", good and evil...
The letter "D" gives us those things that are somewhat more *reliable...*

Death   Destruction   Despair

To "Dust" we shall return...

Doing what is right is what He wants from us...

Do not be tempted by Evil...

Does having the "D" letter in your name give you a little more "Strength" than those without?

Or might it also mean that you are the ones that face more "Drinking" and "Drug" Problems?

Decide for yourself; "Does" every word in our "Dictionary" That begins with the letter "D" represent "strength" in a more significant way?

Determining the outcome of the battle is why you are needed...
(Satan has more souls; the Lord God has stronger ones)

Dying early in life just might be "Due" to the fact some of you with the letter "D" Are Needed Now...

Dedication and Determination is what He is after...

The name "DAVID" begins and ends with the letter "D"!

****

"The Star of David"

The Lord your God has multiplied you, and here you are today, as the stars of heaven in multitude.

May the Lord God of your fathers make you a thousand times more numerous than you are, and bless you as he has promised you!

DEUTERONOMY 1:10-11

COMMONALITY OF THE LETTER "D"

The "D" letter is filled with strength: Good and Evil!

From the "Dachshund" to "Dynasty", the "D" gives us things we can rely on!

*"Dactylology": The use of the fingers and hands to convey ideas,
As in the manual "Alphabet" used by deaf mutes.*

The "Dad" begins and ends with the letter "D"

The "Dandelion", "Daily", the "Dairy" and the "Daisy"

The "Dalai-lama" and the "Dalmatian"

The "Dam" shows strength, as does the "Damned"

The "Damage" done and the "Damsel" in distress...

Is "Danger" strong?

"Dare" is a strong word as is the "Darkness"

"Darn", "Dashing" the "Date" and especially the "Daughter"

The "D" gives us "David" and the "Dawn"

It gives us each "Day"!

The "Daycare Center" and the "Daydream" begin with the letter "D"

*From "Day-labor" to the "Daylight" the "D" is the "Deacon"
And the very "Dead"*

How about the "Dead-end" or the "Dead-eye"

"Deadly" sounds awful strong...

Is there strength in being "Deaf"?

The "Dean" at the College and the "Dearly Beloved"

"Decay" is next in line as is "Deceased"

The "Declaration of Independence" the "Decline" and "Decompose"

The "Decoy", "Decrease" and "Decree" are all words with strength...

All the "D" words in the "Dictionary" represent strength in one form or another.

That is the definition of the "D"!

From "Defect" to "Defend", "Definition" to "Defiance", the "D" is "Definitive"!

"Defying" all the odds, getting your "Degree", "Dejection", "Delay" and "Delete"

"Deliberate" is the "D"

"Deliverance" is the key...

Our "Delusions" and the word "Demand"

The "Devil" and the "Demon" both start with the "D"

Denial: Refusal to grant the truth of a statement.

"Denounce" and "Deny" are two more "D" words...

"Dependable" starts with the letter "D", as does "Deplorable"

What about "Depressed" and "Deprived"

How strong is the "Depth" of your belief...

"Desire" is a "D" word, "Deserving" too..

"Decide" for yourself if the Power of His Letters give us a clue...

Is your "Destiny" in the hands of our Lord God?

"Destroy" speaks for its self, as does "Destruction"

"Determination" is a key, "Devotion" too!

The "Dictionary" also starts, with the letter "D"
How about the "Dinosaur"

"Disappear", "Disappoint", "Disapprove" and "Disarm"
(Might these words "Describe" why the "Dinosaur" no longer exists)?

There is strength in being a "Disciple" of our Lord God.

The "Dynamite" gets its' strength from within...

How much inner strength does it take to face the "Duel"?

&

Last but not least...

The "Almighty Dollar"

The list of the "D" words will "Dismay" you!

****

Nebuchadnezzar the king,
To all peoples, nations, and languages that dwell in all the earth:
Peace be multiplied to you.
I thought it good to declare the signs and wonders that the Most High God
has worked for me.
How great are His signs,
And how mighty His wonders!
His kingdom is an everlasting kingdom,
And His dominion is from generation to generation.

DANIEL 4:1-3

(Does the above scripture look like the Liberty Bell)

It was typed out exactly as it is written in the Bible,
New lines start at punctuation marks.
Or in the case of the longest line it simply starts by running out of room.

Might those that "DO NOT" believe simply "Disappear"?

****

"I call heaven and earth to witness against you this day,
that you will soon perish from the land
which you cross over to possess;
you will not prolong your days in it,
but will be utterly destroyed.

DEUTERONOMY 4:26

REWARDS OF THE LETTER "D"

Dainty:
Delicately beautiful or charming; exquisite.

Dandy:
A man who affects extreme elegance in his clothes and manners.

"Dapple" and "Daring" are also rewards.

Darling:
One who is very dear, the "Daughter" too...

Dauntless:
That which cannot be intimidated or discouraged.

Dazzle:
To bewilder, amaze or overwhelm with.

Dear:
Beloved; loved; precious. Highly esteemed or regarded.

Debonair:
Suave; nonchalant; urbane, affable, and gracious.

He Rewards us with "Decency" and "Decisiveness"
and the ability to "Deduce"

He rewards us for our good "Deeds" and our "Dedication"

He rewards us with those things that are "Delectable" and "Delicious"

Surely, He rewards us with "Deliverance"!

Is "Dependability" our reward?

How about "Deserving"?

"Desire" and "Desirable" are nice rewards as is "Determined"

"Devotion" and the "Diamond" too...

Is turning the "Double play" a reward...

How about the "Dream" or the "Drive" to do better?

51

Dynamic:
Energetic vigorous, forceful.

How many of us have the true strength to refrain from sin,
Thus the small number of rewards...

Remember the "Dictionary" starts with "D"
Read it for yourself!

The LORD GOD is spelled with two D's...

****

"O Lord, to us *belongs* shame of face,
to our kings, our princes, and our fathers,
because we have sinned against You.

DANIEL 9:8

****

Come, and let us return to the Lord;
For He has torn, but will heal us;
He has stricken, but He will bind us up.

HOSEA 6:1

PUNISHMENT OF THE LETTER "D"

Can He punish us "Daily"; of course He can...

He punishes us with the "Dagger" and the "Damage" done...
Is "Danger" punishment or just being left in the "Dark"?
Most certainly we are punished when we are "Damned"

Dastardly: Cowardly and mean spirited.

Dawdle: To waste time by trifling or loitering; linger.

Is being in a "Daze" a form of punishment?

He gives us the "Deadbeat" and the "Dead-end"

"Death"

Debacle:
A sudden, disastrous overthrow or collapse; rout; ruin.

Debilitated:
Tired; worn out.

Decadent:
In a state or condition of decline or decay.

Is "Deceit" a form of punishment?

How many will understand the "Power of our Alphabet"?

Decimate: To destroy or kill a large part of.

He gives us "Decline", "Decompose" and "Decreased"

Decrepit:
Weakened by old age, illness, or hard use.

"Default", "Defeat", "Defective", "Defiant",
"Deficient", "Deficit" and "Defiled"!

Is being "Degraded" a punishment, how about "Dejected"?

Is the "Delay" our punishment or just being "Delinquent"?

53

Delude:
To deceive the mind or judgment of; mislead.

"Demise"   "Demolish"   "Demotion"

Do not "Deny" our Lord God!

"Deplorable", "Depressed" and "Deprived" are
punishments, as well as "Deserted"

"Despair", "Desperate" and "Despise" too...

Destroy:
To ruin completely; to tear down or break up; demolish.

Destruction:
The condition or fact of being destroyed.

Detest:
To dislike intensely; abhor; loathe.

You can be sure the "Devil" is a form of Punishment!

As we continue with the punishments of the "D" letter,
Always remember "Faith" in our Lord God is what is needed.

Devious:
Straying or departing from the correct or proper way.

Diabolical:
Extremely wicked; fiendishly cruel.

Can He make things "Difficult" for us?

Does He just give us the "Dilemma"?

He did punish the "Dinosaur"
Dirty: Soiled as with dirt; grimy; unclean.

From "Disability" to "Disunited;
Those words beginning with the letters D, I, and S are numerous.
Learn them for your own benefit.
(Do not "Dis" Him)

We as mankind tend to sin frequently and without remorse,

The "D" letter shows us the strength of His punishments!

Is "Divorce" a form of punishment?

"Doom" is certainly a punishment, as is being a "Dope"

Is the "Double-Cross" or "Doubt" our punishments?

Might just being "Down in the Dumps" be His way of dealing with us?

Downhearted: Low in spirit; depressed; discouraged.

Is "Dread" "Dreary" or the "Dropout" punishments?

How about "Dull" or "Dumb"?

Is being stuck in the "Dungeon" or being "Duped" His way of punishing us?

Duress:
Constraint by threat; coercion.

Might He give us "Dysfunctional"?

There are many more "D" words for you to
uncover, grab a: "DICTIONARY"

"Doing" what is "Righteous and Good" is what he "Desires"

***

'This decision is by the decree of the watchers,
And the sentence by the word of the holy ones,
In order that the living may know
That the Most High rules in the Kingdom of men,
Gives it to whomever He will,
And sets over it the lowest of men.'

DANIEL 4:17

55

The next several pages are what is written in the:
NEW KING JAMES VERSION of the HOLY BIBLE...

How much has been changed by Mankind, Our Lord God knows...

****

"Now this *is* the commandment, *and these are* the statutes and
judgments which the LORD your God has commanded to teach you,
that you may observe *them* in the land which
you are crossing over to possess,
"that you may fear the LORD your God,
to keep all His statutes and His commandments
which I command you,
you and your son and grandson,
all the days of your life, and that your days may be prolonged.
"Therefore hear, O Israel, and be careful to observe *it,* that it may be
well with you, and that you may multiply greatly as the LORD God of
your fathers has promised you - 'a land flowing with milk and honey'.
"Hear, O Israel: The LORD our God, the LORD *is* one!
"You shall love the LORD your God with all your heart,
with all your soul, and with all your strength.
"And these words which I command you today shall be your heart.
"You shall teach them diligently to your children,
and shall talk of them when you sit in your house,
when you walk by the way, when you lie down, and when you rise up.
"You shall bind them as a sign on your hand,
and they shall be as frontlets between your eyes.
"You shall write them on the doorposts of
your house and on your gates.

DEUTERONOMY 6:1-9

Following is a list of the "Ten Commandments"
as originally written in the NKJV
Look closely at the first two Commandments,
might they be one in the same?
I have listed what I believe to be the "First"

The Ten Commandments

****

'*I am* the LORD your God who brought
you out of the land of Egypt,
out of the house of bondage.

'You shall have no other gods before Me. (The First)
(Delete space here and you have One Commandment)

(The Second) 'You shall not make for yourself a carved image-any likeness
of anything that *is* in heaven above, or that *is* in the earth beneath,
or that *is* in the water under the earth;
you shall not bow down to them nor serve them.
For I, the LORD your God, *am* a jealous God,
visiting the iniquity of the fathers upon the children
to the third and fourth *generations* of those who hate Me,
but showing mercy to thousands,
to those who love Me and keep My commandments.

'You shall not take the name of the LORD your God in vain,
for the LORD will not hold *him* guiltless
who takes His name in vain.

'Observe the Sabbath day, to keep it holy,
as the LORD your God commanded you.
Six days you shall labor and do all your work,
but the seventh day is the Sabbath of the LORD your God.
In it you shall do no work:
you, nor your son, nor your daughter, nor
your male servant, nor your ox,
nor your donkey, nor any of your cattle, nor
your stranger who is within your gates,
that your male servant and your female may rest as well as you.
And remember that you were a slave in the land of Egypt,
and the LORD your God brought you out
from there by a mighty hand
and by an outstretched arm;
therefore the LORD your God commanded you to keep the Sabbath day.

57

'Honor your father and your mother,
as the LORD your God has commanded you,
that your days may be long,
and that it may be well with you in the land
which the LORD your God is giving you.

'You shall not murder.
'You shall not commit adultery.
'You shall not steal.

'You shall not bear false witness against your neighbor.

'You shall not covet your neighbor's wife;
and you shall not desire your neighbor's house, his field,
his male servant, his female servant,
his ox, his donkey, or anything that is your neighbor's.'

"These words the LORD spoke to all your assembly,
in the mountains from the midst of the fire, the cloud, and the thick darkness,
with a loud voice;
and He added no more.
And He wrote them on two tablets of stone and gave them to me.

DEUTERONOMY 5:6-22

(Might this be the "First")?
"You shall not add to the word which I command you,
nor take from it,
that you may keep the commandments of the LORD your God
which I command you.

DEUTERONOMY 4:2

We are constantly trying to do better than, or keep up with the neighbors,
Or we chase after that which is already Married...

Rest for One Day of the Week...

Your Father And Mother Might just be Wrong on Occasion,
This does not mean that you cannot Honor Them...

TEACH THEM...

All ABOUT THE LETTER "D"

You have Strength so use it Well!

You are a "Doctor", a "Dentist", or might you be a "Dermatologist"?
Could you be a "Dancer" or a "Daredevil"?

Are you a "Dad"?
(Teach the Children Well)

Might you be a "Detective", or work for the "Department of Defense"?
Are you studying for your "Degree"?
Do you enjoy going to the "Department" store,
or might you just enjoy "Dessert"?

Do you sit behind a "Desk", or are you out "Doing"?
Might you just believe in doing your "Duty"?
Do you like to "Draw", or just to "Dream"?

Do you have a "Dictionary" or two?
Is the "Diamond" your favorite jewel?
Do you like the "Daffodil" or the "Daisy"?

Do you own a "Dog"?
A "Day" late and a "Dollar" short
Is the "Deuce" your favorite card, or do you prefer the "Dice"
Might you be a Blackjack "Dealer"?

Just "Do" it...

Discover the Power of our Lord God!
Determination and Dedication are yours for the Asking...

Death is common with the letter "D"
Two other letters of our Alphabet also represent significant death,
Do you know which two?

*

The line of life with all enclosed will make you in-disposed.
"Strength" for all to see...
Dashing and Daring are yours to be
With disbelief' death extreme, this the letter "D"

Notes

EVERLASTING & ETERNITY

EVERYTHING

EVERYONE

EVERYWHERE

E

(The Lord rules above, Evil down below, Mankind sitting in the middle)!

EFFECTS "EVERYONE", "EVERYWHERE"
Belonging to or needed on Earth...

ENVY

EXTINCTION!

*E*vil is *E*verywhere on this *E*arth...

*E*ducation comes in many different forms, who are we to judge others...

*E*quip yourself with all the right tools...
*E*arth will not last forever, heaven does...
*E*ach and *E*very one of us play a part...

*E*ntertainment has three "T's", how often does this word lead us to sin...
*E*xpect the unexpected, for the Lord God works in mysterious ways...

*E*xtinction is a form of punishment...
*E*levate to a new level...
*E*xcuses are *E*asy to come by...

*E*nticing others to the sacrifice of Jesus Christ is one of His requirements...
*E*ternity and *E*verlasting are rewards of the letter *"E"*

****

Now the end *has come* upon you,
And I will send My anger against you,
I will judge you according to your ways,
And I will repay you for all your abominations.
My eye will not spare you,
Nor will I have pity;
But I will repay your ways,
And your abominations will be in your midst;
Then you shall know that I *am* the Lord!

EZEKIEL 7:3-4

"For how can I endure to see the evil that will come to my people?
Or how can I endure to see the destruction of my countrymen"?

ESTER 8:6

COMMONALITY OF THE LETTER "E"

EFFECTS "EVERYONE", "EVERYWHERE": "EARTHLY"

The Capitol letter "E" gives us those things, which are;
Belonging to or needed on Earth...

It includes all things in "Our" world.

From "Each" of us to "Evil" the "E" is "Enormous"!

From being "Eager" to the "Eagle", the "Ear", and waking "Early"

The "E" is "Everything"

From "Earning" a living to being at "Ease", the "E" is "Easily" understood...

The "E" gives us the "East" and "Easter"

It gives us "Eating" and the "Eccentric", the
upper "Echelon" and the "Echo"

Do we not need the "Eclipse", "Ecology", "Economics", and "Ecstasy"?

The "E" gives us the Garden of "Eden" and the "Edge"

It gives us "Education" and "Efficiency"

It gives us the "Effort" and the "Egg"

It gives us the "Ego"; it gives us "Either"/Or...

It gives us the "Elastic" and "Elation", the "Elbow" and the "Elder"

It gives us the "Electronics" and it gives us "Elegance"

It gives us the "Elements" and the "Elephant"

It gives us "Elicit", "Eliminate" and the "Eleventh" hour?

It gives us "Embraced" the "Embryo", "Emerald" and "Eminence"

Do We Not Need Our "Emotions"!

****

Therefore He says:
"Awake, you who sleep,
Arise from the dead,
And Christ will give you light."

EPHESIANS 5:14

"Employment", "Employee", and the "Employer" belong here on Earth!

It gives us "Emptiness" and "Enchantment",
"Enclosure" and "Encouragement"

The "E" gives us the "End"

The "E" gives us the "Enemy" and the "Energy"

It gives us "Engagement", the "Engineer" and the "Engine"

It gives us "English" and the "Enigma"

It also gives us "Enjoyment"

Does the "E" give us "Enough"?

Do we not need free "Enterprise", "Entertainment" and "Enthusiasm"?

Entire: Having no part missing or excepted; whole.

Entity: The fact of existence; being.

The "E" gives us the "Entrance" and "Entrapment"

The "Envelope" and the "Environment"

It gives us "Envy" and the "Enzymes"

The "E" is "Epic"

It gives us the "Epicenter" and the "Epicycle"

The "E" gives us "Equality", "Equations" and the "Equator"

Do we not need all the "Equipment"?

It gives us "Erosion" and the "Eruption", and the "Escalator"

Most of all it gives us "Eternity"

The "E" gives us "Ethics" and "Etiology" and even "Etiquette"

"Euphoria" starts with the letter "E", as does the "Euphrates"

The "Evening" and "Everlasting", "Everyone" and "Everything"

Beware though the "E" also gives us "Evil"!

Evolution and "Exact" are "E" words, as is the "Exam"

From "Excellence" to "Extreme" the "EX", words are abundant.

I will save these words for a later chapter...?

Look for yourself all that is of this "Earth"!

Use your "Eyes" and your "Ears"

The "Earth" is "Enormous" it gives us all this and much, much more...

*Will those with the letter "E" in their names, have
to deal with more "Evil" than those
Without it, or might it just give us the tendency
to be a little more "Emotional"?*

****

**how that by revelation
He made known to me the mystery
(as I have briefly written already, by which, when you read,
you may understand my knowledge in the mystery of Christ).
which in other ages was not made known to the sons of men,
as it has now been revealed by the Spirit to
His holy apostles and prophets:**

EPHESIANS 3:3-5

REWARDS OF THE LETTER "E"

Earnest: Determined; "Eager"; Zealous.
Ease: Freedom from pain, worry, or agitation.
Easy: Capable of being accomplished or acquired with ease.
Economical: Not wasteful or extravagant.
Ecstasy: A state of exalted delight.
Edge: A margin of superiority; an advantage.
Educated: Having an education, especially one above the average.
Effective: Having the intended effect; serving the purpose.
Efficient: Acting or producing with a minimum of waste.
Effort: An attempt; especially an earnest attempt.
Elated: To raise the spirits of; excite feelings of pride.
Electric/Electrifying: Emotionally exciting; thrilling.
Elegant/Elegance: Refinement and grace.
Elite: The best or most skilled member of a social group.
Eloquent/Eloquence: Persuasive, fluent, and graceful.
Eminence/Eminent: Towering above others.
Emphatic: Bold and definite in expression or action.
Emulation: Effort or ambition to equal or pass another.
Enable: To supply with the means, knowledge, or opportunity.

"Enchanting", "Encouraging", "Endearment", "Endeavor"

The Rewards Seem "Endless"!

"Endowed", "Endurance", "Energy", "Engaging", "Engrossing",
"Enhancing", "Enjoyment", "Enjoyable", and "Enlightened"!

The rewards are "Enormous" that is the letter "E"!

"Enriching", "Entertaining", "Enthusiastic", "Enticing", "Enviable"

Epitome:
One that is consummately representative or
expressive of an entire class or type.

We are rewarded with "Equality", "Erotic", "Escape", "Especial",
"Essence", "Essentials", "Establishment", and "Esteem"

Can He Reward us with "Eternal" life, of course He can!

He gives us "Ethics", "Etiquette", and "Euphoria"

He rewards us with the ability to "Evade" and "Evoke"

"Exaltation" and the ability to "Examine" are forms of rewards...

Does He reward us with our very "Existence"!

The "E" is a very common letter in our alphabet, ask yourself why?

We as humankind dwell on "Earth",
The "E" gives us all those things belonging to or needed here on this planet...

You must remember though "Evil" starts with the
letter "E" thus making it very strong.

Refraining from sin will "Entitle" us to all the rewards of the letter "E"

It seems like He would like to reward us?

As with the Rewards He gives to us, the Punishments are just as "Enormous"!

Try to remember as we get started,
That the Lord God not only asks us to believe in Him,
But what also is required by us;

Is to ask for forgiveness and to "do our best" to refrain from sinning,
And to spread the word of the Sacrifice of our Savior "Jesus Christ"

****

But to each one of us grace was given according
to the measure of Christ's gift.

EPHESIANS 4:7

PUNISHMENTS OF THE LETTER "E"

Can He punish "Each" and "Everyone" one of us!

He punishes us with the "Earache", and the "Earthquake"

How about the "Eavesdropper"?

Ecocide:
Deliberate destruction of the natural environment, as by pollutants.

He punish us with "Eczema" and being "Edgy"

Efface: To rub or wipe out; obliterate; erase.
Effete: Unable to produce further offspring or fruit; barren.
Effort: A difficult or tiring exertion of strength or will.

Is the "Ego" a form of punishment or how about "Electrocution"?

He punishes us with the "Elements"

Are the "Embargo" or "Embarrassment" forms of punishment?

Embattle: To dispose to struggle or resist.

Will He punish those that "Embezzle"?

Is "Emphysema" a form of punishment or just feeling "Empty"?

Encroach:
To intrude gradually or insidiously upon the domain, possessions,
Or rights of another; trespass.

Encumber: To weigh down unduly; lay too much upon.

Is the "End" our ultimate Punishment?
Or is having to "Endure" the Wrath of our Lord God our Punishment?

****

"Then the Egyptians shall know that I *am* the Lord, when I have
gained honor for Myself over Pharaoh, his chariots, and his horsemen".

EXODUS 14:18

Does He punish us with the "Enormity" of the situation?
Or does He simply not give us "Enough"?

Are "Enslave", "Entangle", "Entrap" and "Envy" the way
He gives us our punishments?

Ephemeral: Lasting for a brief time; short lived; transitory.

The "Epidemic" is a strong form of punishment...

He gives us "Erosion", "Erosive", and the "Err",
"Errand" and "Errant", "Erratic" and the "Error"

The "Eruption" could be a form of punishment?

Is being "Estranged" His form of punishment?

"Exaggeration" and the "Excuse" are "E" letters as well as the "Execution"

"Exhaustion" too...

"Enjoy" this life He has given to us...

"Educate" yourself to our Lord God...

Protect the "Environment" and remember "Evil" does "Exist"!

****

And you, fathers, do not provoke your children to wrath,
but bring them up in the training and
admonition of the Lord.

EPHESIANS 6:4

The Lord rules Above, Evil below,
Mankind in the middle' which way will you go?
"Explore" the Power of the "Earthly" E,
Learn the difference Between You and Me!

ALL ABOUT THE LETTER "E"

"Except" the Responsibility...

You could be into "Education" or Protecting the "Environment"?
Are you an "Electrician" or might you be an "Expert" on the "Economy"?
Might you be in the "Entertainment" Industry or an "Engineer"?

Are you "Easy" to get along with or might you be a little "Evil"?

"Enjoy" the "E" for it gives you "Everything"!

Could it be that you might just be an "Egghead"?

"Ego" begins with the letter "E"

Is your favorite number, "Eight" or "Eleven"?

Does the "E", "Excite" you?

Might you just like to "Experiment"?
Could it be that you are an "Entrepreneur"?
Do you believe in "Evolution"?

Are you "Eager" to learn?

Clean your "Ears" and "Eat" well...

Keep your "Eyes" open and you will see our Lord God!

"Experience" His return...

Find faith in our Lord God and life will be made; "Everlasting"!

****

"And now for a little while grace has been
***shown* from the LORD our God,**
to leave us a remnant to escape, and to
give us a peg in His holy place,
that our God may enlighten our eyes
and give us a measure of revival in our bondage.

EZRA 9:8

FAITH & FORGIVENESS

FAMILY

FRIENDS

FOOD

FAME

FORTUNE

F

The Capitol Letter "F"
All our /His "Favorite things...

(Not much Evil down below)

FAKE

FOOL

FORNICATION?

71

Find the Lord God in your own way...

Feel His power...

Forget what you have been taught...

Faith is what you need...

Focus on the letters...

Forever is His reward...

****

But I want you to know, brethren,
that the things *which happened* to me have actually
turned out for the furtherance of the gospel, so that it
has become evident to the whole palace guard,
and to all the rest, that my chains are in Christ;
and most of the brethren in the Lord, having
become confident by my chains,
are much more bold to speak the word without fear.
Some indeed preach Christ even from envy and strife,
and some also from goodwill:
The former preach Christ from selfish ambition, not sincerely,
supposing to add affliction to my chains;
but the latter out of love,
knowing that I am appointed for the defense of the gospel.
What then?
Only *that* in every way, whether in pretense
or in the truth, Christ is preached;
and in this I rejoice, yes and will rejoice.

PHILIPPIANS 1:12-18

***

"Faith" and "Forgiveness" are "Favorites" of His
So little evil in any of this!
Christ fed many with little "Fish"
The "Fake" and the "Fool" spoil the Dish.

COMMONALITY OF THE LETTER "F"

Our favorite things; His favorite things.

Fable: A story about legendary persons and exploits...

The "Faucet" and the "Face-lift"

The "Facilities" to get things done...

Having all the "Facts"

Working at the "Factory"

Factotum: An employee or assistant who serves in a wide range of capacities.

Might we just enjoy going to the "Fair"?

Ask the golfer he will tell you the "Fairway" is one of his favorite things...

Do we desire "Fair-trade" and "Fair-weather"?

How about the "Fairy Tales"?

There is little doubt "Faith" is one of our Lord Gods favorite things...

Is "Fame" one of our favorite things?

Or is it just for things to be "Familiar"?

Surely our "Family" is a favorite thing to have...

How about the "Fan";
(The ones who fill the seats or even the one that keeps the room cool)

All the "Fancy" things...

Is getting the "Fanfare" one of your favorite things...

The "F" is Fantastic!

It gives us our "Fantasies" and very "Far-away"

The "Farm" and the "Farmer" just might be one of our Lords favorite things?

The "F" gives us "Fascination" and even "Fashion"

The word "Favorite" begins with the letter "F"

It gives us the "Fawn" and the "Faze" we go through...

The "Feast" and the "Feather" are "F" words, as is the "Featured" event...

"Feedback", "Feelings", and the "Fellow man" all start with the "F"

How about "Fellowship" and the "Female" too...

The "Fences" give us our privacy...

"Fermentation"

How about the "Fern" the "Ferret" or the "Ferry"

Being "Fertile" has lots of advantages...

Is going to the "Festival" a favorite of yours?

How about teaching the dog to "Fetch"?

What is your favorite "Fetish"?

The "Fetus" might be one of His favorite things, might the "Fig" also?

The "Fiction" novel seems to be quite popular...

Playing in the "Fields" was one of my favorite things...

"Figment" of our imagination is an "F" word...

Do we desire a nice "Figure" or just for the "Files" to be where we left them?

Might having "Five Fingers" be His favorite?

Our LORD GOD Will
"Finish-First"

The "Camp-Fire" and the "Fireplace" are two
of my favorites the "Fireworks" too...

"Fishing"

"Fitting" in...

The American "Flag"

The "Flattery" and the "Flavor"

The "Flesh" seems to be something the Lord enjoys...

"Flexibility" and the ability to "Fly"
"Flirting" and the ability to "Float"

Ask the farmer he will tell you the "Flock" is his favorite...

What would we do without the "Floors"?

"Florist", "Flossing", "Flour", and the "Flowers" are all "F" words.

We definitely enjoy the "Fluids"

To be able to "Flush" the toilet...

Keeping your "Focus"

Our "Folks"

"Follow" the path of our Lord God!

"Food" is for sure a favorite...

The things that are "Forbidden"

The correct "Forecast"

How about our "Forefathers"

The "Foreigner"
(They make America what it is today)...

"Forensics" and the ability to "For-see" the future...

The "Forest" has to be on the top of the list...

"Fornication" too...

"Fortune" is something we all seem to desire...

The "Four H" clubs...

The "Four-leaf clover"

The "Franchise" player...

The "Fraternity"

Its "Free"

"Freewill"

"Freedom" is something we all desire...

The ability to "Freeze"

The "Freight"

How about the "French Fries"

"Fresh"

The "Frog" seems to be fairly important in our evolutionary cycle...

How about the wild "Frontier"?

Does He enjoy the morning "Frost"?

The "Frosting" on the cake is one of my favorite things...

So is the "Fruit"

Fruition: Enjoyment derived from use or possession.

**Forgive those who do not understand, do not judge.
Let them be judged by the LORD!**

"Fuel" seems to be high up on our list...

The desire to be "Funny"

*Ask a member of our "Armed Forces", they will
tell you the "Furlough" is a favorite...*

Is the "Furniture" one of your favorites?

"Fusion" seems to be important...

A "Future" with the Lord God is something we should all desire!

Look up all those "F" words that I have left out and decide for yourself...

"Follow" in the path of our Lord God and all the rewards will be yours...

****

**Therefore, my beloved and longed-for brethren,
my joy and crown,
so stand fast in the Lord, beloved.**

PHILIPPIANS 4:1

****

*Fishing one evening I prayed to the Lord,
Bring me a fish for to purchase I cannot afford!
In the distant rain cloud far away' a great whale began to sway,
His mouth wide open' for a large fish like this I was a hope-in...
Soon came three little fish in the sky to play'
Into the great mouth they did stray,
Guess how many fish I took home that day?*

REWARDS OF THE LETTER "F"

He rewards us with the "Facilities" to get the job done...

He rewards us with the "Facts"

Faculty: An inherent power or ability.

He rewards us with "Fairness" and with "Faith"

Faithful: Worthy of trust or credence; consistently reliable

Is "Fame" a form of reward?

Familiarity: Having fair knowledge of something; acquainted.

Is the "Family" a wonderful reward?

Is being "Fanciful"?

Fantastic: Wonderful or superb; remarkable; uncanny

He rewards us with our "Fantasies"

Fascinating: Arousing interest as by charm or beauty; captivating.

Fastidious: Careful in all details; exacting; meticulous.

How about becoming a "Father"

Faultless: Without fault; blameless or flawless.

Surely, the Lord God looking at us "Favorably" is a reward!

Feasibility: Capable of being accomplished or brought about.

He rewards us with the "Feast" and being able to accomplish the "Feat"

He rewards us with "Feelings"

Is "Fellowship" our reward, or being able to "Fend" for ourselves?

Is "Fertility" a form of reward, or being in a "Festive" mood?

Finesse:
Artful restraint and delicacy of performance or behavior.

He rewards us with being able to "Finish" the task at hand...

Is being able to stand "Firm" in our beliefs a form of reward?

First: Ranking above all others in importance or quality; best.

Is being "Fit" for the task or being in "Fit" condition, rewards?

Flair: A natural talent or aptitude; knack.

He rewards us with "Flamboyance" and "Flair"

Might the "Flattery" be our reward?

Flexibility: Responsive to change; adaptable.
Flourish: To fare well; succeed; prosper.
Focus: To produce a clear image of; to concentrate on.

"Focus" on the letter "F", the Rewards are numerous...

Follow: To accept the guidance or leadership of.

Follow the path of our Lord God and you will be rewarded with:

Fondness: Warm affection; tender liking; strong preference.
Forbearing: Tolerant; patient.
Forethought: Deliberation, consideration, or planning beforehand.

"Forgiveness" has to be a Reward!

Are we rewarded with the ability to "Formulate"?
Or are we rewarded with "Fortitude"?

Might just being "Fortunate" enough to get to Heaven be our reward?

Is it the ability to move "Forward" that is His way of rewarding us?

Foxy: Suggestive of a fox; sly; cunning; clever. (Or a pretty woman).
Frank: Open and sincere in expression; straightforward.

Surely, "Freedom" is a Reward...
Is having a "Fresh" start a reward, or just having a "Friend"?

How about the "Fringe" benefits?

Frisky: Energetic, lively, and playful.

Frolic: A gay, carefree time.

Is being in the "Front" of the line a reward?

"Fulfillment" is our reward, as is having "Fun"

The ability to "Function" and learning the "Fundamentals"
Are His way of rewarding us...

As is being "Funny"

The Lord God gives us our "Future" as a Reward...

"Find" "Faith" and All the Rewards Will Be Yours!

****

"This people honors Me with their lips,
But their heart is far from Me.
And in vain they worship Me,
Teaching as doctrines the commandments of men.

MARK 7:7

"And whenever you stand praying,
if you have anything against anyone, forgive him,
that your Father in heaven may also
forgive you your trespasses.
"But if you do not forgive,
neither will your Father in heaven forgive your trespasses.

MARK 11:25-26

Are we such a "Foolish" Kingdom that we cannot see **His** *signs?*

PUNISHMENTS OF THE LETTER "F"

Fabrication: Something as a deliberate false statement.
Factious: Lacking authenticity or genuineness; sham.

"Failure" is a Punishment as is "Faithless" the "Fake" too...

Fall: To be cast down; be defeated or overthrown.
False: Contrary to fact or truth, without grounds, incorrect.
Falter: To waver in confidence; hesitate.

Is "Famine" a punishment or the "Fanatic", how about the "Farce"?

Fatal: Causing or capable of causing death; mortal.

Is "Fatigue" a form of punishment?

Fatuity: Stupidity conveyed with an air of pride or self-satisfaction.
Fault: Something that prevents perfection.
Faze: To disrupt the composure of; bother; disconcert; disturb.

"Fear" is surely a form of; as is the "Fee" we are required to pay...

Feign/Feint: To give a false appearance of; pretend: to sham.
Fell: Able to destroy; lethal.
Feud: A bitter prolonged hostility between two families Individuals or clans; vendetta.

Is the "Fever" a form of punishment or just having to "Few"?

Fictitious: Nonexistent; imaginary; unreal.
Fiend: A diabolically evil or wicked person.

Is the "Fight" a form of punishment, or just being "Filthy"?
Is the "Fine" we pay our punishment, or just being "Finicky"?

Flagrant: (The flagrant foul seems like a form of punishment)
Flam: A lie or hoax; deception.
Flaunt: To exhibit ostentatiously; show off.
Flaw: An imperfection; a blemish or defect.

Do we choose to "Flee" from our Moral Obligations to the Lord God?
Or do we just lack the Understanding?

WILLIAM E. BEAVERS

"Find" the Lord God in "Your Own Way".
I have found him through the letters of the
Alphabet and in the Clouds from Above!
(A Visit from Peter, Paul, and John did not hurt Either)

Flog: To beat harshly with a whip or rod.

Is the "Flood" a punishment or just being a "Flop"?

Flounder: To move clumsily; as to regain balance.
Flub-dub: Pretentious nonsense, especially in argument.

Is the "Flu" His way of punishing us or does He give us the "Fluke"?

Is the "Flurry" of the wind?

Might the "Fly" be a punishment for not keeping things clean?

Fogy: A person of old-fashioned habits; outmoded attitudes.

Is being a "Fool" a form of punishment?

Fop: A vain, affected man who is preoccupied with his clothes and manners;
a dandy.
Foray: A sudden raid or military advance.

Adam was "Forbidden" to eat from the tree of life,
Was Mankind not punished for his Sins?

Forfeit: Something surrendered as "Punishment" for a crime.
Forgetful: Neglectful; thoughtless; careless.
Foul: Offensive to the senses; disgusting; revolting.
Fracas: A disorderly uproar; noisy quarrel; brawl.
Frantic: Emotionally distraught, as from fear, pain, or worry.
Frazzle: To wear out the nerves of.
Frenzy: A seizure of violent agitation or wild excitement.
Fret: To cause to be uneasy; distress; vex.
Frigid: Lacking warmth of feeling; stiff and formal in manner.
Frump: A dull, plain, unfashionably dressed girl or woman.

Is being "Frightened" a form of His punishment?

"Frustration", "Furious", "Fussy" and "Futile" are also punishments...

Does He "Frown" upon Us when we sin, of course He Does!

82

ALL ABOUT THE LETTER "F'

Are you a "Family Practitioner" or a "Firefighter"?
Might you work for the "Federal Government",
the "FBI" or the "Federal Reserve"?
Are you a "First- sergeant", "First-mate", how about a "First-lieutenant"?
Are you a "Fighter" in the "Flyweight" or "Featherweight" division?

Might you play "First" base?
Are you the "First" born?
Do you like to "Fish"?
Do you just like having all the "Facts"?
Might you be "Famous"?
Are you a "Father"?
Do you "Fear" the unknown?
Are you sometimes "Forgetful" or do you like driving "Fast"?
Might you just like to "Finish" what you start?
"Fix" it...
Are you a little "Flaky" or do you have "Flair"?
Does it seem like you always catch the "Flu"?
Is the "Fourth" of July your favorite time of the year?
Are "French Fries" or "French Toast" your "Favorites"?
Or do you just enjoy "Food" of all kinds...

Try not to get to "Fat"

There is an "F" for you
And remember that you are related to the letter "P"

"FIND" "FAITH" IN THE "LORD GOD"
AND LIFE WILL BE "FANTASTIC"

****

I thank my God,
making mention of you always in my prayers,
hearing of your love and faith which you have toward the
Lord Jesus and toward all the saints,
that the sharing of your faith may become effective by the
acknowledgment of every good thing which is in you in Christ Jesus.
For we have great joy and consolation in your love,
because the hearts of the saints have been refreshed by you,
brother.

PHILEMON 1:4-7

GODS WORLD

GUARANTEED

GREAT

GHOSTLY

G

The Life and Times of the Lord God...

GUILT

GREED

"Guess" what is next?

Go forth and multiply...
(Read Luke 21:23)

Give to those in need...

Guarantee yourself a place in Heaven...

Guess where Greed will lead you to...

Great are His Rewards...

Glorify His Name...

****

" May God Almighty bless you,
And make you fruitful and multiply you,
That you may be an assembly of peoples;
And give you the blessing of Abraham,
To you and your descendants with you,
That you may inherit the land In which you are a stranger,
Which God gave to Abraham."

GENESIS 28:3-4

The word "Giving" begins and ends with the letter "G"!
(Gods World: The word "Gift" begins with the "G" and ends with the "T")

Maybe this year instead of buying a lot of expensive gifts for your loved ones
Try getting together as a family and donate your
efforts to helping those less fortunate...

This should include the Churches too, Double the effort...

COMMONALITY OF THE LETTER "G"

The letter "G" gives us the "Life Of" our LORD GOD!

Gad: To roam about or ramble restlessly; to rove.

To "Gain" the trust of others...

The word "Galaxy" speaks for itself as does the "Gale" force wind...

The sea of "Galilee" sounds "Godly" to me...

How about "Gallant", the "Galleon" and the "Gallery"?

Gallivant: To roam about aimlessly or frivolously; traipse.
Galvanize: To arouse to awareness or action; to spur; startle.

A life without the Lord God is a big "Gamble"!

Can the "Gang" be godly?
(Teach our children well and the answer is Yes)

Gantlet:
A section of, "overlapping" but "independent" railroad track.

Gap: A suspension of continuity; interval.

Does the "Garage" door retrace its path?

Does the "Garbage" tend to reappear, or might it just be a punishment?

Does He enjoy the "Garden"?

Do you understand the letter "G"?

We sometimes feel that our Lord God is not always with Us,
Does the fact that He has the capitol "G" give us an indication Why?

Does the Bible tell us about the "Garnishment" we must pay for our debts?

The "Gates" of Heaven are surely "Godly"

The "Gathering" of the disciples has to have been "Godly"

"Gender" and the "Gene", and the ability to "Generate"

How about "Genetics"?

The word "Gentile" is used by many believers...

Germ: A small organic structure or cell from which a new organism may develop. (Sounds like the work of God to me).

Gestation: The period of carrying developing offspring in the uterus after conception; Pregnancy.

The word "Ghost" speaks for itself...

Giant: A person or thing of extraordinary size or importance...

Gibbet: An upright post with a crosspiece, forming a T-shaped structure from Which executed criminals were hung for viewing.

"Get out", "Get up" "Get together" and live with the Lord God...

The "Gill" sounds like something from God...

What about the "Giraffe"? Or the "Ginseng"?

Girandole: A composition or structure in "radiating" form.

Gird: To encircle, to surround.

Give: To make a present of; bestow.

Is the "Glacier" part of our Lord Gods world?

Certainly the "Girl" is...
Support your Girl Scouts!
The Boy Scouts too...

Are you starting to understand the letter "G" yet?
"Go back" and check out some of the words I have left out!
(Might that be a clue)?

Have you noticed how the "G" letter fits with the Lord God?

Glaring: Staring fixed and angrily. (Definitely our Lord God here)!

Gleam: A steady but subdued shinning; a glow.
Glean: To gather grain left behind by reapers.

Glide: To move in a smooth, effortless manner.
Glint: A momentary flash of light, a sparkle.

The word "Globe" seems to just about cover it...

The "Glove" protects our hands...

"Gloria" sounds like a nice name...

"Glorious" is certainly with the Lord God...

"Glowing" sounds like Him...

How about the "Gnat" the "Gnome" or the "Gnu"

Goal: The purpose toward which an endeavor is directed.
(He does have a goal for us)

How about "Gold"

Golden rule: The maxim of teaching that one should behave towards others
As one would have others behave toward one self.

"Goliath" starts with the letter "G", as does the city of "Gomorrah"

Good Samaritan: In a New Testament parable,
The only passer-by to aid a man who had been beaten and robbed.

"Gospel" starts with the "G", as does "Government"

Gown: A long, loose, flowing garment, as a robe or nightgown.

Grace: Seemingly effortless beauty or charm of movement.

The "Grail" starts with a "G" as does "Grain" and "Grand"

The "Grape", "Grass", "Grateful", "Gratitude", and the "Grave"

How about "Gravity"?

Let us not forget the "Grandfather" and the "Grandson"

The very "Ground" we walk on...

How about the "Guarantee" or the "Guardian"?

Let the LORD GOD be your "Guide"!

****

And as many as walk according to this rule,
peace and mercy be upon them, and upon the Israel of God.
From now on let no one trouble me,
for I bear in my body the marks of the Lord Jesus.
Brethren, the grace of our Lord Jesus
Christ be with your spirit.
Amen

GALATIANS 6:16-18

"GLORIFY HIS RETURN"

God is the "G", in the dictionary' this you will see!
Go to those words that you know'
To heavens-gate is where it will lead.
The double "EE' in the word greed,
Punishments to those not from His seed...

(And remember the punishments can be given
to third and fourth generations)

REWARDS OF THE LETTER "G'

Gaily: In a joyful, cheerful, or happy manner; merrily.
Gain/Gainful: To secure as profit, or through labor; earn.
Gallant: Attentive to women; chivalrous; daring; valorous.
Gamy: Showing an unyielding spirit; plucky; hardy.
Gay: Showing or characterized by exuberance or excitement.
Gem: A beloved or highly prized person.
Generous: Willing to give or share; unselfish.
Genial: Having a pleasant or friendly disposition or manner.
Gentle: Considerate or kindly in disposition; amiable; patient.
Genuine: Free from hypocrisy or dishonesty; sincere.

Gift: A gift from the Lord God is certainly a reward...
Is the "Giggle" a form of reward?
Surely, the ability to "Give" is a reward...

Glad: Experiencing or exhibiting joy and pleasure.
Glide: To move in a smooth, effortless manner.
Glow: To shine brightly and steadily; as with pride.
Godsend: An unexpected boon or stroke of luck; windfall.
God-speed: Success, or good fortune.

"Golf" starts with the letter "G"

All those words that start with "Good" seem like nice rewards!

Gorgeous: Dazzlingly brilliant; resplendent; magnificent.
Gracious: Characterized by kindness and warm courtesy.

The "Grand Slam" sounds like a nice reward...

Is the ability to "Grasp" that, which is in front of you a reward?

"Grateful", "Gratifying", and "Gratuity" sound like nice rewards...

Pass the "Gravy" please…

Great:
Remarkable or outstanding in magnitude, degree; or extent:
Significant; important; meaningful; noble; excellent!

All those words that start with the word
"Great" have a nice ring to them...

Is the "Grin" a nice reward or just having the
"Grit" to stick with your beliefs!

Is being a "Groom" a form of reward?
Is the ability to "Grow" a reward?

Guiltless: Free from guilt; blameless; innocent.
Gusto: Fondness; taste; liking; vigorous enjoyment; zest.
Gutsy: Full of courage; daring; plucky.

The name "God" has the capitol "G" therefore;
He uses the "G" to distinguish Himself to Us...

Are we ready or willing to move forward in a
more clear life with the Lord God?

The letters of the "Alphabet" will help us to
understand the way our Lord God works...

Are you still a little skeptical?

No one has the right to demand that you believe;
"Belief" is yours and yours alone to find.

It is my wish, that by explaining the letters of the Alphabet,
That you too will become closer to the Lord.

****

"God, who made the world and everything in it,
since He is Lord of heaven and earth,
does not dwell in temples made with hands.
"Nor is He worshiped with men's hands,
as though He needed anything, since
He gives to all life, breath, and all things.
"And He has made from one blood every nation of men to dwell
on all the face of the earth,
and has determined their preappointed times
and the boundaries of their dwellings,
"so that they should seek the Lord,
in the hope that they might grope for Him and find Him,
though He is not far from each one of us;

ACTS 17:24-27

PUNISHMENTS OF THE LETTER "G'

Gabby: Tending to talk excessively.
Gaffe: A clumsy social error.
Gag: Any obstacle to or censoring of free speech.
Gall: Something bitter to endure; Impudence.
Gash: A deep flesh wound; a long deep cut.
Gaunt: Thin and bony; emaciated and haggard; drawn.

Were the "Gangster", "Gangplank", or the "Gas Chamber" forms of punishment?

Was the "Gauntlet" a form of punishment?

Gawk: An awkward loutish person; oaf.
Ghastly: Terrifying; dreadful.
Gimmick: A device employed, often illegally, to cheat or deceive.
Gloom: Dismal, dark, dreary; sadden.
Glum: In low spirits; dejected; dismal.
Gone: Dying or dead, ruined; lost.
Goof: An incompetent, foolish, or stupid person.
Goon: A thug hired to commit acts of intimidation or violence.
Gory: Covered or stained with blood; bloody; bloodstained.
Gossip: Trifling, often-groundless rumor; idle talk.
Graze: A scratch or abrasion resulting from contact.

Greed: A rapacious desire for more than one needs or deserves.

How about the "Gridlock"?

Grim: Uninviting or unnerving in aspect; forbidding; terrible.
Gripe: To complain, nag or grumble.
Grouchy: Inclined to grumbling and complaint.

"Grudge", "Gruesome", "Grumpy", "Guilt" and the "Guillotine"

****

**"And behold, I am coming quickly, and My reward *is* with Me,
to give to every one according to his work.
I am the Alpha and the Omega, *the* Beginning
and *the* End, the First and the Last".**

REVELATION 22:12-13

ALL ABOUT THE LETTER "G"

Are you into "Gardening"?
Might you work for "General Motors" or "GE"?
Could you own a "Garage"?
Are you into "Genealogy"?

Could you be a "Gypsy", or are you always the "Gentleman"?
Do you work the "Graveyard" shift or are you just "Grateful" for the things you have?
Is your favorite color "Green" or "Gold", or how about "Grey"?

Do you own a "Grill"?
Do you own a "Gun"?

Do you work at the "Grocery Store"?
Is "Geometry" your favorite subject?
How about "Geography"?

Do you own a "Gallery" or just enjoy visiting?
Might you be a professional "Gambler"?
Or maybe you just enjoy playing "Games"?

Do you enjoy "Giving" or are you just "Glad" to be alive...
Surely, you do not enjoy mowing the "Grass"?
(Might you smoke it)?

"Guess" where belief will lead you?

Do you own or just like going to the "Gym"?
"Glory" starts with the letter "G", as does "Gorgeous"?

"God" is a "G" word...

****

Have you suffered so many things in vain-if indeed it *was* in vain?

Therefore He who supplies the Spirit to you and works miracles among you,
***does He do it* by the works of the law, or by the hearing of faith?-**
just as Abraham *"believed God, and it was*
accounted to him for righteousness"
Therefore know that *only* those who are of faith are sons of Abraham.

GALATIANS 3:4-7

Notes

HEAVEN

HAVE

H

(There we are again (Mankind), sitting in the middle).

Heaven or Hell, either/or? Both...

HAVE NOT

HELL

Which Will You Chose?

97

How Hard is the letter "H"?

Heaven...

Hell...

History repeats itself...

Have we forgotten...

His return will be glorious...

Help is on the way...

Hide...

****

**By faith the walls of Jericho fell down after
they were encircled for seven days.
By faith the harlot Rahab did not perish with those who did not believe,
when she had received the spies with peace.
And what more shall I say?**

**For the time would fail me to tell of Gideon
and Barak and Samson and Jephthah,
also *of* David and Samuel and the prophets:
who through faith subdued kingdoms,
worked righteousness,
obtained promises,
stopped the mouths of lions,
quenched the violence of fire,
escaped the edge of the sword,
out of weakness were made strong,
became valiant in battle,
turned to flight the armies of the aliens.**

HEBREWS 11:30-34

"Hurrah"   *"Hurrah"*

COMMONALITY OF THE LETTER "H'

The Capitol letter "H" words give us a choice between Heaven and Hell...

It is that simple, Right or Wrong; Good or Evil; Black or White; Positive or Negative. (Notice that each of the opposite words have the same amount of letters)?

Is this just coincidence?

The "H" represents for us; "Choices" between, Or might it simply give us those things that can be Either/Or?

The "Home" or the "Hospital" a "Hero" or a "Hobo", "Handsome" or "Homely", The list continues...

Understand that for all our common "H" words you too can find one that leans on the Side of Good and one that leans toward the negative side, All can be Either Heaven or Hell...

Remember there is good and evil in all things...

Does this also include the letters of our "Alphabet"?

OF COURSE...

Have we have spent too much of our lives studying the Numbers and not Enough Time with the Letters of our Alphabet?

The Language we know and study, dates back thousands of years...

We as children of the Lord God probably need to slow down just a touch and Reconsider all those things in life, which are truly important...

Anyway, back to the Capitol letter "H"

I will list numerous words of the letter "H", Both positive words and what I believe to be those that lead towards the side of Negativity...

There will be numerous others that you might want to enjoy figuring out...

Spend some time with a loved one and have "Fun"

Our Lord works in mysterious ways; learn while you still can...

"Have" or "Have not", "Harmful" or "Harmless", "Help" or "Hinder",
Are just a few...

Is there a negative word for "Hail", how about
"Hell", or might it be the word "Hot"

Use your "Imagination" if you are an "I"; use your "Wisdom" if you are a "W",
And use the "T" to "Think" if you have the "T"

All of our letters are important; All do give us good and evil;
(So find the Lord God and enjoy the rewards)!

Could the negative of "Handsome" be the "Hobo"?

Could the negative of "Handful" be, "Hand-out"?

How about if we choose to give someone a "Helping Hand",
Or could the negative be to "Handcuff" a person?

"Handicraft/Handy-work" or "Handicapped"?

Is "Hardy" the negative of "Hardly", or could it be the word "Hard"?

The "H" "Halfway" between Good and Evil,
We get many, many words that give to us; Either/Or...

Heart: Emotional constitution, disposition, or mood;
Capacity for generosity or sympathy, compassion;
Love; affection; Inner strength, loyal or courageous; Fortitude;
The essence of.

Which might be the negative?

"Heartache", "Heartbroken", or how about the "Heart attack"?

"Hear" or "Hearsay"?
"Headfirst" or the "Headache"?
"Heavy" or "Hollow"?
"Here" or "Hereafter"?
"Heal" or "Hurt"?
"Him" or "Her"?
(Choose wisely)

Understanding the letter "H" is yours to find...

Might you be able to find a different or better word for its opposite?

Could the opposite of "History" be the "Hoax"?

Hoist: To raise or haul up.
Hoe: To dig down.

Homonym: One of two or more words that have the same
sound and often the same spelling but differ in meaning.
Homograph: A word that is spelled the same as another word but
differs in meaning and origin and may differ in pronunciation.
Homophone: A word having the same sound as another but differing from its
Origin, spelling, or meaning.

"Honesty" or "Hypocrite"?
"Hopeful" or "Hopeless"?
"Heaven" or "Horror"?
"Hemisphere" or "Horizon"?
"Headstrong" or "Humble"?

The letter "H" gives us many examples of opposites...

My wish is only to show you the similarities,
To get you to think about the possibilities of the powers of the Alphabet.

Does having the "H" letter in our name give us
a better ability to decide between,
Or does it mean that we will have more choices to make?
Could it give us the ability for both?

****

Therefore, as the Holy Spirit says:

"Today, if you will hear His voice,
Do not harden your hearts as in the rebellion,
In the day of trial in the wilderness,
Where your fathers tested Me, tried Me,
And saw My works forty years.
Therefore I was angry with that generation,
And said,
'They always go astray in their hearts,
And they have not known My ways.'
So I swore in My wrath,
"They shall not enter My rest."

HEBREWS 3:7-11

REWARDS OF THE LETTER "H"

Halo:
A luminous ring or disk of light surrounding the head or bodies of sacred figures,
As of saints.

Is the ability to use our "Hands" a form of reward?
Or just the ability to "Handle" the Responsibilities He gives to us?

Handsome:
Pleasing and dignified in form or appearance;
Generous; liberal; proficient; compatible.

Happy:
Characterized by luck or good fortune; prosperous:
Having or demonstrating pleasure or satisfaction; gratified.

Hardy: Stalwart and rugged; strong, courageous, stouthearted.
Harmony: Agreement in feeling, approach, action, disposition.

Is the "Harvest" a form of His Reward?
Or might it be the "Hatchery"?

Is the ability to "Have" His Reward to each of us?

How about the ability to use our "Heads"?

Surely, the ability to "Heal" is a reward?

Healthy: Possessing good health; Indicative of a
rational or constructive frame of mind.

The ability to "Hear" and the "Heart" could be His way of Rewarding us...

How about "Heat"?

"Heaven" is surely our reward!

Heedful: Paying close attention; taking heed; mindful.

He gives us the "Heirloom" as a form of reward...

He gives us the "Help" when we need it...

Heroic: Having or displaying the qualities of a hero, courageous.

Is the ability to "Hide" a form of reward?

High-spirited: having a proud or unbroken spirit, brave.

Does He Give Us A "Hint"?

There are clues in the Alphabet "and" in the Dictionary!

Is the ability to "Hold" on to what we have, a form of reward?

How about the "Holiday"?

Holy:
Belonging to, derived from, or associated with a divine power;
Sacred, worthy of worship or high esteem.

Is the "Home" our reward or might it be the "Home-made" pie?

Honesty: Not lying, cheating, stealing or taking unfair advantage of.
Honor: Esteem; respect; reverence, glory; fame; distinction.
Hope: To look forward to with confidence or fulfillment.

Is each "Hour" of the day our reward?

How about the "Hug"?

Humdinger: Someone or something extraordinary or superior.

Is "Humor" a form of reward?

Is the "Husband" a reward?

Is good personal "Hygiene" its own reward?

Hymn: A Song of Praise or Thanksgiving to the Lord God.

Imagination and Understanding are the skills it
takes to comprehend His message to Us.

Halfway: Midway between two points or conditions; in the middle.
Halve: To separate or divide into two equal portions or parts.

The Capitol (H), gives us "Heaven" and "Hell", both paths are wide open...
Mankind lies in the Middle, Between Good and Evil.

Which path will you choose?

PUNISHMENTS OF THE LETTER "H"

Hag: An ugly, frightful old woman, a witch; sorceress.
Haggard: Appearing worn and exhausted; gaunt; uncontrolled.
Hallucination: Any false or mistaken idea; delusion.
Hamper: To prevent the free movement, action or progress of.

Was/Is the "Hanging" a form of His punishment?

How about the "Hangover"?

Harass: To disturb or irritate persistently; to wear out; exhaust.

He does make things "Hard" for us as our punishment...

Is "Hate" a form of punishment?

Havoc: Destruction, as caused by a natural calamity or war.
Hazard: A chance or accident; a danger; peril.
Heinous: Grossly wicked or reprehensible; abominable; vile.

He can make things "Heavy" or "Hectic" as forms of His punishments...

"Hell" is definitely a form of His punishment!

Hesitate: To be slow to act or decide; reluctant; waver.
Hex: An evil spell; a curse; a bad influence on.
Hinder: To obstruct or delay the progress of; prevent; to stop.
Hoity-toity: Arrogant; pompous; pretentious.
Hollow: Without substance or character; empty; superficial.

Was the "Holocaust" a form of punishment?

Horrible/Horror: Intense dislike; unpleasant; disagreeable.

"Hostile" and "Hostility" sound like punishments?

Is "Hunger" a form of punishment?

He gives us the "Hurdles" to overcome...

Is listening to all the "Hype"?

Highs and lows are in the letter "H", how many will you be able to find?

ALL ABOUT THE LETTER "H"

Do you teach at the "High School"?
Do you work at the "Hospital"?
Might you Raise or Race "Horses"?

Do you enjoy cleaning the "House", or might you just like to stay at "Home"?

"Have" and "Have-not" are issues with you...

Do you farm "Hay"; do you know "How"?
Might you just work "Hard"?

Is the "Hamburger" one of your favorites?

"Hope" begins with the letter "H"

Are you a creature of "Habit"?
Might you be a little "Headstrong"?

"Humor" is yours to give...

Is "History" your favorite subject, or might you teach it...

Read your "Horoscope"

"Heaven" and "Hell" are Our Two Choices!

****

His brightness was like the light;
He had rays *flashing* from His hand,
And there His power *was* hidden.
Before Him went pestilence,
And never followed at His feet.
He stood and measured the earth;
He looked and startled the nations.
And the everlasting mountains were scattered,
The perpetual hills bowed.
His ways *are* everlasting.
I saw the tents of Cushan in affliction;
The curtains of the land of Midian trembled.

HABAKKUK 3:4-7

INCONCEIVABLE
Or
INCREDIBLE

Inspirational

Intelligence

I

Ignorance

The Invasion or Incapable of...

INJURED

IMPOSTER!

Introduce yourself to the Lord, start your day with a prayer...

If you believe...

It will happen...

Investigate...

Is this real?

Interpret...

Individually...

Instruct others...

Insist on getting all the facts...

****

Now it shall come to pass in the latter days
That the mountain of the Lord's house
shall be established on the top of the mountains,
And shall be exalted above the hills;
And all nations shall flow to it.
Many people shall come and say,
"Come and let us go up to the mountain of the Lord,
To the house of the God of Jacob;
He will teach us His ways,
And we shall walk in His paths."
For out of Zion shall go forth the law,
And the word of the Lord from Jerusalem.
He shall judge between the nations,
And rebuke many people;
They shall beat their swords into plowshares,
And their spears into pruning hooks;
Nation shall not lift up sword against nation,
Neither shall they learn war anymore.

ISAIAH 2:2-4

COMMONALITY OF THE LETTER "I"

The letter "I" gives us a look at ourselves;
It gives us an "Invasion" into our very minds...

To our Lord God, the "I" represents an:
"Invasion", "Interruption" in life or maybe not?

Are you willing to learn more about the letter "I"?

Our most used words that begin with the letter "I" gives us that "Interruption",
"Invasion" in our own lives or it gives us those words that make it "Impossible"!

Does the word "Ice" fit into this definition, let us
use the "Imagination" for a moment...

"Imagine" how "Ice" has changed our lives...
"Ice" cold drinks, the "Ice" pack, frozen foods etc...

The "Ice-age" was an "Interruption" of life...

The "Idea" could be an "Invasion/Interruption" in our minds...

Ideal: A "Conception" of something in its absolute perfection.

Identical: Developed from the same ovum.
(Was there a second "Invasion" or "Interruption" into the ovum)?

Identity/Identification: An invasion of our privacy?

Do we use other "Idols" to invade our time with the Lord God?

If: used to "introduce", indicating.

Do not "Ignore" the facts...

Can falling "Ill" be an invasion or interruption to our health?

Illation: The act of "inferring" or drawing conclusion to.
Illegal: An invasion or interruption of our laws.
Illusion: An erroneous "perception" of reality.

Is the "Image" we perceive an invasion of our minds?

If we "Imitate" another, are we not "invading" who they are?

109

Is being "Immeasurable" a non-interruption?
If we do something "Immediately", does this not interrupt our time?

Immerse: Completely submerged in water. (Is this an interruption of our air supply)?
Imminent: About to occur; impending. (Sounds like an interruption about to incur)?
Immobile: Unable to move. (No interruption/invasion here)?
Immortal: Not subject to death. (No interruption of life)?
Immovable: Incapable of being moved.
Immune: Not affected. (No invasion or interruption here)?

"Impact" "Impale" "Impartial" "Impassioned" "Impatient"
"Impeach" "Impeccable" "Impede" "Impenetrable" "Imperative"
"Imperfect" "Impetuous", all fit this same definition...

How about the "Implant", (an invasion into our bodies)?

Implication: To "involve" intimately or incriminatingly.
Imply: To "involve" or "suggest"; to hint.
Import: To bring or carry in from an "outside" source.
Impose: To obtrude or "force" upon another or others.

The word "Imposter" sounds like an invasion of our identity?

"Impotent" "Impound" "Impractical" "Impregnate"

Are you "Impressed" yet?

"Improbable" "Improper" "Improve" "Improvise" "Impulsive".
"Inaccurate" "Inactive" "Inadequate" "Incapable" "Incapacitate"

Can all these words involve an interruption/non-interruption in some form or another?

"Is" and "If" both, start with the letter "I"

How about the word "In"?

Do you see the possibilities of these words?
How deep can we go?

Incisive: Cutting; "penetrating"
Incident: A definite, distinct occurrence; tending to occur.

If we "Include" things into our minds;
Is that not an interruption/invasion into our very thought process?

How about the word "Income",
Do we not constantly battle with the interruptions/invasions of?

"Income-tax", this sure invades my pocketbook...

"Incoming" speaks for itself...

Incomprehensible: Incapable of being understood or comprehended; unknowable.
(No interruption here)!

"Incomplete" sounds invading...

"Inconsequential", "Inconsiderate" and "Inconsistency" are "I" words...
As are "Inconvenient" and "Incorrigible"

"Independent" sounds like a word without much interruption?
As do "In-depth" and "Indeterminable"

Does the "I" letter give us an "Indication"?

Have we not invaded the "Indian" and the "Iraq's"!
How about "Iran" or "India"?
(Let us not forget; "Iwo-Jima")

The letter "I" gives us an abundance of words that fit into the definition mentioned.
Either with or without interruption; all our most common words
beginning with the "I" Gives us the glimpse of the power of this letter.

Incomprehensible: Incapable of being understood or comprehended; unknowable;
unfathomable; without limits.

Incursion: A sudden attack on or invasion of hostile territory.

****

I will punish the world for *its* evil,
And the wicked for their iniquity;
I will halt the arrogance of the proud,
And will lay low the haughtiness of the terrible.

ISAIAH 13:11

Indeed: Without a doubt; certainly; truly.
Indefeasible: Not capable of being annulled or made void.
Indefensible: Not capable of being defended.
Indefinable: Not capable of being defined, described, or analyzed.
Indelible: Incapable of being removed, erased, or washed away.
Indescribable: Incapable of description; indefinable.
Indestructible: Not capable of being destroyed; unbreakable.
Indeterminate: Not capable of clear interpretation; inclusive.
Indivisible: Incapable of being divided.
Inevitable: Incapable of being avoided or prevented.

"Infest" and "Infiltrate" sound like invasions?

Infinite: Having no boundaries or limits; Unlimited.
Inflexible: Incapable of being changed; unalterable.

Can the "Information" we receive be an invasion to our minds?

If we "Infringe" on another are we not invading their space?

"Inject" sounds like an invasion?

Does the end of each "Inning" in baseball give us an interruption?

Is "Innocence" free from the invasion?

Does the "Insect" invade our lives?

Does "Insomnia" invade our sleep?

Does the "Insult" invade our feelings?

"Intermittent" sounds like it is full of interruptions...

Interrupt: To break in upon an action or discourse.

Is the "Intersection" an interruption of our drive?

Is the "Interstate" free from interruption?

Interval: A space between two objects, points or units.
Intervene: To come, appear, or lie between two things.

Is "Intimacy" without interruption?

If we become "Intoxicated" is that not the alcohol invading our system?

The word "Intrude" speaks for itself...

Is "Intuition" an invasion of our thinking or might it be a reward?

"Invade" starts with the letter "I", as does "Interruption"!

Invulnerable: Incapable of being damaged, injured, or wounded.

"Irregular" sounds like it is full of interruptions...

Irrupt: To break or burst in; make an incursion or invasion.

The "Island" is invaded by water on all sides...

Does the "Itch" give us an invasion?

The letter "I", either full of invasions/interruptions or incapable of!

Does the letter "I" also make us think about ourselves?
(As in Me, Myself, and "I")

****

**Is it not yet a very little while Till Lebanon
shall be turned into a fruitful field,
And the fruitful field be esteemed as a forest?
In that day the deaf shall hear the words of the book,
And the eyes of the blind shall see out of
obscurity and out of darkness.
The humble also shall increase *their* joy in the Lord,
And the poor among men shall rejoice In the Holy One of Israel.**

ISAIAH 29:17-19

REWARDS OF THE LETTER "I"

"Ice Cream" sounds like a nice reward...

How about the "Icing" on your favorite cake?

Ideal: A conception of something in its absolute perfection.

Is the ability to "Identify" right from wrong a reward?

Illuminate: To provide with, or focus light upon; to make understandable; to enlighten.

Is the "Imagination" a form of his rewards?
(Do those without an "I" in their name have less)?

Immaculate: Free from fault or error; spotless; pure.

Is the ability to act "Immediately" a form of reward?

"Immortal" sounds like a reward from our Lord God...

How about "Immunity"?

Impassion: To arouse the passions of.
Impeccable: Without flaw; faultless; not capable of sin.
Important: Carrying a great deal of weight or value; significant.

Is the ability to "Impregnate" a reward, or is it the ability to "Impress" others?

Impressive: Commanding attention; awesome or stirring.

How about the ability to "Improve"?

Improvise: To invent, compose, or recite without preparation.

Incentive: Something inciting to action or effort;
As the fear of "punishment" or the expectation of "reward".

Does the Lord God "Include" us in His world as a form of reward?

Is the "Income" a form of reward?

If we "Increase", our family is that our way of being rewarded?

Is being "Independent" a reward?

Does he give us "Individuality" as a reward?

Is the ability to "Indulge" in our desires a form of reward?

Industrious: Diligently active; assiduous in work or study.

Is the "Infant" our reward?

Is the ability to "Influence" or "Inform" others a reward?

Ingenuity: Inventive skill or imagination; cleverness.

Could knowing the "Ingredients" to your favorite recipe be a reward?

Is "Inheritance" our reward or is it the ability to take the "Initiative"?

Is the "In-law" a reward or a punishment?

Innocent: Uncorrupted by evil, malice, or wrongdoing; sinless.
Inspiration: Stimulation of the faculties to a high level of feeling.
Inspire: To affect, guide, or arouse by divine influence.

Have I been "Inspired" to write what I believe!

Following in the path of righteousness will give
you the "Inspiration" you need...

Instinct: A powerful motivation or impulse.

Do we use our "Instincts" to keep us out of harms way?
(Sounds like a nice reward)

Integrity: Rigid adherence to a code of behavior; unimpaired.
Intellect: The ability to learn and reason; to think profoundly.
Intelligence: The capacity to acquire and apply knowledge.
Intensity: Exceptionally great concentration, power, or force.
Intentions: An aim that guides action; a design.

Following through with our "Intentions" is not always easy...

Can Finding Faith in the Lord God make those things Easier for Us?

He gives us the ability to "Invent", and to "Invest"
our money as forms of reward...

Is being "Intriguing" a form of reward?

Is the "Invitation" a form of reward?

Invoke: To call upon a higher power for assistance.

Father:
We Pray Today, Tomorrow, And Tonight, that you may Enlighten Us...

Is being "Involved" a Reward or is it the ability to look "Inward"?
(How Awesome Is He)

He Sees "Inside" Each One of Us...

The letter "I" is "Intriguing":
Will Having the "I" in our name give Us more "Intelligence"?
Or might it give us "Ignorance"?

How often do you tend to "Interrupt"?
(The Double "RR")

Will Finding Faith in the Lord God;
Strengthen Us from the "Invasion/Interruption" into our lives,
Or will it divide us?

Involving Yourself in the "Word" of God is the Answer...

"Inspect" the Power of "His" letters...

"Interact" with "Others"

I Believe!

The Lord above' evil below, no sign of man' what does it Mean?
The Indian and the Iraqi are two of your clues'
Are they paying their just dues?
"Invasion" or not, both ways are seen.
Imagination' Impossible' Infinity and "I"
The letters from our Lord will not lie!

****

"For as the new heavens and the new earth
Which I will make shall remain before Me,"
says the LORD,
"So shall your descendants and your name remain.
And it shall come to pass
That from one New Moon to another,
And from one Sabbath to another,
All flesh shall come to worship before Me,"
says the LORD.
"And they shall go forth and look
Upon the corpses of the men
Who have transgressed against Me.
For their worm does not die,
And their fire is not quenched.
They shall be an abhorrence to all flesh."

ISAIAH 66:22-24

****

And in that day you will say;
" O LORD, I will praise you;
Though You were angry with me,
Your anger is turned away,
and You comfort me.
Behold,
God *is* my salvation,
I will trust and not be afraid;
'For YAH, the LORD, *is* my strength and song;
He also has become my salvation.'"

ISAIAH 12:1-2

All that He is looking for is "Improvement"
I therefore will continue His work...

How many will interpret the letters in the wrong ways?

PUNISHMENTS OF THE LETTER "I"

Is being an "Idiot" a form of punishment, how about if we sit by "Idly"?

Surely, "Ignorance" is a form of punishment...

When we fall "Ill", is that a Small form of His punishment?

"Illegal" "Illegible" "Illegitimate" "Illicit" "Illiterate"

Impair: To diminish in strength, value, quantity, or quality.

Is "Impatience" a form of His punishment?

"Impeach" sounds like a punishment...

Impede: To obstruct the way of; block.

"Imperfect" speaks for itself...

Impersonal: Not personal; not related or connected to anyone.
Impetuous: Impulsive, brash, rushing with violence.
Impinge: To collide; strike; dash.
Implosion: A more or less violent collapse inward.

"Impose" and "Impound" too...

Do not fall for the "Imposter"!

****

**And I saw one of his heads as if it had been mortally wounded,
and his deadly wound was healed.
And all the world marveled and followed the beast.
So they worshiped the dragon who gave authority to the beast;
and they worshiped the beast,
saying,
"Who *is* like the beast?
Who is able to make war with him?"**

REVELATION 13:3-4

Might being "Impotent" be a form of punishment?

When was the last time you had your car "Impounded"?

"Impoverished", "Impractical", "Imprisoned",
Improper", "Impulsive", "Impure"

The List of the punishments beginning with the letters "I-n" are "Insane"
(Look Them Up in the Dictionary with a Friend or Loved one)
(Read between the Lines, Read those words You know)

Irrational:
Affected by loss of usual or normal mental clarity; contrary to reason; illogical.

Do not be "Irrecoverable"

Are you sometimes "Irregular"?
"Irresponsible" begins with the letter "I"
Are you a little bit "Irritated"?

Do you feel a little "Isolated" about now?

You have been "Issued" a warning...

Does it "Itch"?

He Does Have an "Itinerary"!

****

Therefore the Lord says,
The LORD of hosts, the Mighty One of Israel,
"Ah, I will rid Myself of My adversaries,
And take vengeance on My enemies.
I will turn My hand against you,
And thoroughly purge away your dross,
And take away all your alloy.
I will restore your judges as at first,
And your counselors as at the beginning.
Afterward you shall be called the city of
righteousness, the faithful city."

ISAIAH 1:24-26

ALL ABOUT THE LETTER "I"

"Investigator" and "Insurance" start with the letter "I"

Do you like lots of "Ice"?

What Flavor of "Ice Cream" is your Favorite?

The "Icing" on the Cake...

Try "Ice-skating"

Might you be full of "Ideas"?

Use Caution, you could be a victim of "Identity-Theft"

Do not sit by "Idly"

"Idolize" Him...

Are you in the "Industrial" Business?

Do you sometimes fall "Ill"?

"Imagine" the possibilities...

"Immigration Service" and the "Inventor"

Have you been a victim of "Incest"?

"Invest" wisely...

"Influence" Others to our Lord and our Savior...

I'm "Innocent"

"In" one ear and out the other...

"Insist" on knowing all the Facts...

*Might you tend to "Ignore" those around you
or do you just "Interrupt" them?*

JUDGMENT DAY

JUSTICE

J

The Life and Times of our Savior Jesus Christ...

Jacob Joshua Jeremiah James Joseph John

Juvenile

Jealousy *is* a punishment...

Join His team...
Jacob...
James...
Jeremiah...
Jerusalem...
Jews...
Joel...
John...
Jonah...
Joseph...
Joshua...
Judah...

"Joan of Arc", and Judas...

****

Beloved, while I was diligent to write to you
concerning our common salvation,
I found it necessary to write to you exhorting you to contend
earnestly for the faith which was once for all delivered to the saints.
For certain men have crept in unnoticed,
who long ago were marked out for this condemnation, ungodly men,
who turn the grace of our God into lewdness and deny the only
Lord God and our Lord Jesus Christ.

JUDE 3-4

But I want to remind you, though you once knew this, that the Lord,
having saved the people out of the land of Egypt,
afterward destroyed those who did not believe.

JUDE 5

COMMONALITY OF THE LETTER "J"

The "life" of our Lord and Savior Jesus Christ
The letter "J" will show us the life of "Jesus";
it gives us a Clue into His world!

Jab:
To poke abruptly, especially with something sharp.
(Was "Jesus" pierced by the Spear)?

Jacal:
A thatch-roofed hut made of wattle and daub.
(Was this in the time of "Jesus")?

Jack:
A man; fellow; chap: One who does odd or heavy jobs; a laborer.

Jackal:
A doglike carnivorous animal.

Jackass:
A male Ass or Donkey.

Jacket:
A short coat, hip length, worn by men and women.

Jackpot:
To experience great success or sudden good fortune.
(He saved "All", what a jackpot that must have been).

The "Jackrabbit"

Jackstay:
A stay for cruising vessels used to steady the mast against the strain of the gaff.

Jackstraw:
A game played with a pile of straw or thin sticks.

"Jacob" sounds like a godly name...

Jake:
Fine; suitable; all right.

Jam:
There is that food thing again...

James:
The Twentieth book of the New Testament, also one of the Twelve Apostles.

Jamboree:
A noisy celebration, a large assembly; a mass gathering.

Jar:
An earthenware vessel with a wide mouth and usually without handles.

Jaunt:
A short trip or excursion, usually pleasurable; an outing.

Javelin:
A light spear thrown with the hand and used as a weapon.

Jaw:
The walls of a pass or canyon; cavern

Jawbone:
To urge voluntary compliance with "official" wishes or guidelines.

Jean:
A heavy strong twilled cotton used in making clothing.

"Jeremiah"

"Jerusalem"

****

**Keep yourselves in the love of God,
looking for the mercy of our Lord
Jesus Christ unto eternal life.**

JUDE 1:21

Jersey:
A soft plain knitted fabric used for clothing.

Jeroboam:
A wine bottle holding about 4/5 of a gallon,
Named after "Jeroboam I"; who made Israel to sin.

Jess:
A short strap fastened around the leg of a hawk or other bird.

Jet:
A dense black coal that takes a high polish and is used for jewelry.

Jetty:
A pier or other structure projecting into a body of
water to influence the current or tide,
Or protect a harbor or a shoreline.

Jew:
A descendant of the Hebrew people.

Jib/Jibe
That boat thing again...

Did He enjoy the "Jitterbug"?

Joan of Arc:
The "Patron Saint"

He did His "Job"

How about the word "Jockey"?

Joel:
A Book of the Old Testament, containing the
prophecies of the judgment of "Judah"

The name "John" has a definite religious impact...

"Join" the team...

How many thought of the teachings of Jesus as a "Joke"?

Jolly:
Full of merriment and good spirits, gay, cheerful, festive.

"*Jonah*"   "*Joseph*"   "*Joshua*"

Journal: The Bible!

"Journey" with Him...

Joust:
A combat with lances between two; a tournament.

Jubilee:
*In the Old Testament, a year of rest to be observed
by the Israelites every 50th year.*

Judah:
Ancestor of one of the Twelve Tribes of Israel.

Judas:
One of the Twelve Apostles.
(Saint Jude)

Judge:
To sit in judgment upon; to try; hear.

JUDGMENT DAY
The Day of Gods final Judgment...

****

**'Perhaps everyone will listen and turn from his evil way,
that I may relent concerning the calamity which
I propose to bring on them because of the evil of their doings.'**

JEREMIAH 26:3

Judicature/Judicial/Judiciary/Judicious

Jug:
A small pitcher made for holding liquids, usually with a stopper or cap.

Did He enjoy the "Juggler"?

The word "Jump" has many definitions...

Meet Him at the "Junction"

The word "Jungle" starts with the "J"

As does "Junior"

"Jurisdiction"   "Jurisprudence"

The "Juror" and the "Jury"

Just:
Honorable and fair in one's dealings and actions.

Justice:
Moral righteousness, equity, honor, fairness.

"Justify" His sacrifice...

Juvenile:
How Young Was He?

****

But the LORD said to me:
"Do not say, 'I *am* a youth,'
For you shall go to all to whom I send you,
And whatever I command you, you shall speak.

JEREMIAH 1:7

***

Journey through the letter "J" teach others what "Jesus" had to say,
The life and times of our Savior released'
when all the common words are pieced!

Judge me not without your knowing my heart'
judge me not that is the start.
Looks deceive and the mind plays tricks'
but with Jesus Christ this boy sticks!

REWARDS OF THE LETTER "J"

Jackpot:
A top prize or Reward.

Jaunty:
Crisp and dapper in appearance; having a buoyant
or self-confident air; brisk; carefree.

Are the "Jewels" and the "Jewelry" forms of His rewards?

Jocular:
Given to good-humored joking; merry.

Jolly: Full of merriment and good spirits; fun loving.
Josh: To tease, good-humor; to joke.
Jovial: Marked by hearty conviviality.

Surely "Joy" is a form of reward...

Joyful/Joyous:
Feeling, causing, or indicating joy.

Jubilation:
A celebration or other expression of joy.

Might He just give us good "Judgment"?

"Just"

The ability to "Justify" our actions...

****

And the Jews marveled, saying,
"How does this Man know letters,
having never studied?"

JOHN 7:15

129

PUNISHMENTS OF THE LETTER "J"

Jabber: To utter rapidly or unintelligibly, or idly.
Jackass: A foolish or stupid person, blockhead.

Do not let His work become "Jaded"

Might "Jail" be a form of punishment?

Jargon:
Nonsensical, incoherent, or meaningless utterance; gibberish

Jaundice:
Affected by envy, jealousy, prejudice, or hostility.

"Jealousy" is a punishment...

Stop being such a "Jerk"

Jeer:
To speak or shout derisively, mock.

Jezebel:
A scheming wicked woman.

Do not put a "Jinx" on me...

Jitter:
To be nervous or uneasy; to fidget.

Is having to deal with all the "Junk" His way of punishing us?

Does the "Junkie" have a hard time living in mans world?

Are there few "J" words because "Jesus" lived a short life?

Just ask yourself if all of this is making "any" sense to you?

(That is the Start)

****

Hear this, you elders,
And give ear, all you inhabitants of the land!
Has *anything like* this happened in your days,
Or even in the days of your fathers?
Tell your children about it,
Let your children *tell* their children,
And their children another generation.

JOEL 1:2-3

*****

"Only be strong and very courageous,
that you may observe to do according to all the law which
Moses My servant commanded you;
do not turn from it to the right hand or to the left,
that you may prosper wherever you go.
"This Book of the Law shall not depart from your mouth,
but you shall meditate in it day and night,
that you may observe to do according to all that is written in it.
For then you will make your way prosperous,
and then you will have good success.
"Have I not commanded you?
Be strong and of good courage;
do not be afraid, nor be dismayed,
for the LORD your God is with you wherever you go."

JOSHUA 1:7-9

ALL ABOUT THE LETTER "J"

Just because you have the letter "J" does not mean
you always use good "Judgment"
You could work for the "Justice Department" or might you be a "Janitor"?
Might you work as a Carpenter or be in the Construction business?
(Jesus was a Carpenter)

Pass the "Jelly" and the "Jam"

"Jewelry"?

Do you know a good "Joke" when you hear it?
Or might you be the one always telling them?

"Just Do It"

How much time have you spent in "Jail"?
Are you the "Jealous" type?

Do you always wear "Jeans"?
"Joy" belongs to you...

"Juice", "Jujitsu", "Judo" and the "Julep" begin with the letter "J"
Are you into "Junk Bonds", or might there be
lots of "Junk" around the house?
Journey into His world...

Do not "Judge", lest you be "Judged"

And remember you are related to the letter "G"

"Just" when we thought we knew it all...

****

My brethren, count it all joy when you fall into various trials,
knowing that the testing of your faith produces patience.
But let patience have *its* perfect work,
that you may be perfect and complete, lacking nothing.
If any of you lacks wisdom, let him ask of God,
who gives to all liberally and without reproach,
and it will be given to him.
But let him ask in faith, with no doubting,
for he who doubts is like a wave of the sea
driven and tossed by the wind.
For let not that man suppose that he will
receive anything from the Lord;

JAMES 1:1-7

Notes

KINDNESS
KIDS &
KNOWLEDGE

K

"Deceitful"
(Deceit is not always a negative thing)

KILLER   KIDNAPPER

Kindness can be given for the wrong reasons...

Kids can be a wonderful reward...

Knowledge can be deceitful...

Know the power of our Lord God...

Keep spreading the word of Jesus Christ...

****

"So if you walk in My ways, to keep My
statues and my commandments,
as your father David walked, then I will lengthen your days."

1 KINGS 3:14

"And I will dwell among the children of Israel,
and will not forsake My people Israel."

1 KINGS 6:13

"*But* if you or your sons at all turn from following Me,
and do not keep My commandments *and* My statues which I have
set before you, but go and serve other gods and worship them,
"then I will cut off Israel from the land which I have given them;
and this house which I have consecrated for
My name I will cast out of My sight.
Israel will be a proverb and a byword among all peoples.

1 KINGS 9: 6-7

And Jehoash said to the priest, "All the money of the
dedicated gifts that are brought into the house of the Lord-
each man's assessment money-*and* all the money that a man
purposes in his heart to bring into the house of the Lord,
"let the priests take *it* themselves, each from his constituency;
and let them repair the damages of the temple,
wherever any dilapidation is found."

2 KINGS 4-5

COMMONALITY OF THE LETTER "K"

Deceitful!

Deceit is not always a negative thing...

The "Kaleidoscope" produces many beautiful patterns and colors...

Where we deceived by the "Kamikaze" planes?

*The "Kangaroo" is deceitful in its strength, ability
to jump, and the hidden pouch...*

Do you know how much that "Karat" you are wearing is worth?

"Karate"   "Kung Fu"   "Karma"

*The "Katydid" has **deceptive** organs in the wings that produce sound...*

*The "Kayak" is **deceptive** in its speed and agility...*

The word "Keel" sounds like the word "Kill"

What is the value of you favorite "Keepsake"?

How much is left in the "Keg"?

Do we know all the uses for "Kelp"?

"Keno" looks easier than it actually is...

The "Kernel" looks fairly useless until planted...

How about the word "Kerosene"?

What's cooking in the "Kettle"?

Where did I leave my "Keys"?

The "Key" looks like it should fit...

"Khaki" is a camouflage used to deceive...

The "Kick" has deceit in its power...

Kid: To deceive in fun; to fool.

Watch-out for that Kid!

How deceitful does the "Kidnapper" have to be?

The "Killer" uses deceit of all kinds...

*How about the "Kilt" or the "Kimono" looks like
they should be worn by women...*

The "Kindergartner" is smarter than you think...

The "Kindling" will start a roaring fire...

Is the "King" (President) always honest with us?

Kink: A slight difficulty or flaw; a quirk of personality.

How deceiving can that first "Kiss" be?

*Kite:
Did you know what you could do with some sticks and paper?
In business, any negotiable paper representing a fictitious transaction.*

"Kleptomaniac"

What is in that "Knapsack"?

Knavery: Dishonest or crafty dealing, trickery.

The "Knife" was sharper than it looked...

Are you "Knitting" a sweater or might it be a blanket?

"Knock", "Knock", who is there?

The "Knock-Out" punch...

**Kindle the fire' strike up the band' the letter "K" is at hand.
With this comes "Kindness", "Kids", and "Knowledge";
Where will you learn this in college?
Do they teach about "Deceit", or how the "Lord" we shall meet!**

The "Knot" does not look so tough to untie...
"Knowledge" can be deceitful...
Ask the ballplayer, he will tell you the "Knuckleball" is full of deceit...
"Korea", "Ku Klux Klan", "Kuwait"

****

"When Your people Israel are defeated before an enemy
because they have sinned against You,
and when they turn back to You and confess Your name,
and pray and make supplication to You in this temple,
then hear in heaven, and forgive the sin of Your people Israel,
and bring them back to the land which You gave to their fathers.
"When the heavens are shut up and there is no rain
because they have sinned against You,
when they pray toward this place and confess Your name,
and turn from their sin because You afflict them,
"then hear in heaven, and forgive the sin of Your servants,
Your people Israel,
that you may teach them the good way in which they should walk;
and send rain on Your land which You have
given to Your people as an inheritance.
"When there is famine in the land,
pestilence *or* blight *or* mildew, locust *or* grasshoppers;
when their enemy besieges them in the land of their cities;
whatever plague or whatever sickness *there is*;
"whatever prayer, whatever supplication is made by anyone,
or by all Your people Israel,
when each one knows the plague of his own heart,
and spreads out his hands toward this temple:
"then hear in heaven Your dwelling place,
and forgive, and act,
and give to everyone according to all his ways,
whose heart You know
(for You alone know the hearts of all the sons of men),
"that they may fear You all the days that they live in the land
which You gave to our fathers.

1 KINGS 8:33-40

REWARDS OF THE LETTER "K"

Might that "Karat" on your finger be a reward?

Keen: Intellectually acute; penetrating; sharp; vivid; strong.

Is the ability to "Keep" what we have a form of His rewards?

How about the "Keepsake"?

The ability to have "Kids" is a reward...

Being "Kind" is its own reward...

Kindle: To arouse; inspire.

The "Kiss" sounds like a reward?

Knack:
A clever expedient way of doing something: A specific talent,
Especially one difficult to explain or teach.

Being crowned a "Knight" Sounds rewarding...

The ability to "Knit"

Know:
To perceive directly with the senses or mind;
apprehend with clarity or certainty.

Know the truth...

The beginning of "Knowledge" is fear of the Lord...

"Kudos" to you...

****

And in their mouth was found no deceit,
for they are without fault before the throne of God.

REVELATION 14:5

PUNISHMENTS OF THE LETTER "K"

Might being "Killed" be a punishment?

Killjoy: A person that spoils the enthusiasm or fun of others.

Kink: A painful muscle spasm, as in the back or neck; a crick.

Klutz: A clumsy or dull witted person; a bungler.

Know-it-all: A person who arrogantly claims to know everything.

Know-nothing: An ignoramus; an anti-intellectual.

Do not be such a "Kook"

Is dealing with the "Koran" a Punishment for all Christians?

"Kryptonite" was a punishment for Superman...(Learn to smile)

The letter "K" gives us a unique shape in our language:
The significance of this seems to be fairly important...

As we dive deeper into the "letters" you too might come to understand why...

"Knowledge" is a wonderful thing...

"Kids" too...

****

Josiah *was* eight years old when he became king,
and he reigned thirty-one years in Jerusalem.
His mother's name *was* Jedidah the
daughter of Adaiah of Bozkath.
And he did *what was* right in the sight of the LORD,
and he walked in all the ways of his father David;
he did not turn aside to the right hand or to the left.

2 KINGS 22:1-2

ALL ABOUT THE LETTER "K"

"Kind-a" sounds like the letter "C"

"Can" you deal with it?

"Crazy" huh...

"Careful" what you wish for...

Might you have the "Killer" instinct?

Be "Kind"

The "Caretaker" has the letter "K"

What's the deal with the "Ketchup"?

"Kin" are next in line...

"Quick" what is next?

The letter "Q"

"Quintessential"

"Questions" remain...

He is "Crafty"

"Catch" Him if you "Can"

"Quit" sinning...

He is playing for "Keeps"!

****

**Now these were the heads of the mighty men whom David had,
who strengthened themselves with him
in his kingdom, with all Israel,
to make him king, according to the word
of the LORD concerning Israel.**

1 CHRONICLES 11:10

Having made it through to the letter "L", things
now become quite Extraordinary!

****

"Therefore I speak in parables, because
seeing they do not see,
and hearing they do not hear, nor do they understand.
"And in them the prophecy of Isaiah is fulfilled,
which says:

"Hearing you will hear and shall not understand,
And seeing you will see and not perceive;
For the hearts of this people have grown dull.
Their ears are hard of hearing,
And their eyes they have closed,
Lest they should see with their eyes and hear with their ears,
Lest they should understand with their hearts and turn,
So that I should heal them.'

MATTHEW 13:13-15

Notes

LORD

LIFE

LOVE

LETTERS

LANGUAGE

L

Life made easier, tough at the beginning...
(Tough Love)

LOOK OUT BELOW....

LUST   LIAR   LAZY   LUCIFER

Lest you be terrified...

Little did I know...

Learn the Letters...

Love thy Neighbor...

Lust is a sin...

Look out below...

Live His Life...

Let the "Lord God" be your Leader...

****

"The Spirit of the Lord is upon Me,
Because He has anointed Me
To preach the gospel to the poor;
He has sent Me to heal the brokenhearted,
To proclaim liberty to the captives
And recovery of sight to the blind,
To set at liberty those who are oppressed;
To proclaim the acceptable year of the Lord."

LUKE 4:18-19

"And there will be signs in the sun, in the moon, and in the stars;
and on the earth distress of nations, with
perplexity, the sea and the waves roaring;
"men's hearts failing them from fear and the
expectation of those things which
are coming on the earth, for the powers
of the heavens will be shaken.
"Then they will see the Son of Man coming in
a cloud with power and great glory.
"Now when these things begin to happen,
look up and lift your heads,
because your redemption draws near."

LUKE 21:25-28

COMMONALITY OF THE LETTER "L"

The letter "L" gives us those words in our "Language" that have the tendency to Make Our lives somewhat easier; Is there less evil in the little "l"?

"Life Made Easier":
(There is a "lot" of tough "love" at the start with the capitol "L" however)

Look up for yourself in the Dictionary
All those "L" letter words that are "Common"
To You...

Divide By three...

Either they will fall into "Commonality":
(Those things in life that make it just a little
easier; tough at the beginning)
Or
Rewards and Punishments...

"Learn" your "Lessons" for today...

Make a "List"

Might it be a little tough to read the "Label";
However once done it does make it easier...

Will all our "L" words that fit into "Commonality"
fit this same unique pattern?

Labor: Strive for a purpose;
Such work considered as supplying the needs of a community.
(Tough to do the work, yet upon completion it
makes ours and others lives easier)

How tough its it to work in the "Laboratory"

It is tough to lay down the "Lacquer"
(Once done however)

It is a little tough to climb the "Ladder"
(It makes it easier to reach what we are after)

It can be tough to be a "Lady"
(The rewards are worth it)

Owning "Land" makes life easier...

Be careful of the "Landing"

How tough is it to find the "Landmark"?
(It helps us locate where we are)

Tough to locate the "Land-mine"!
(A sigh of relief when found)

Tough to do the "Landscaping"!
(Very nice when completed however)

Discovering the secrets of our "Language"!
(How much easier might life become)?

Tough to light the "Lantern"
(Makes it easier to see)

Learning to make a "Lariat" can be tough!
(Makes it easier to "Lasso" what we are after)

Doing the "Laundry" gives us clean clothes at the end...

Cleaning the "Lavatory"

Mowing the "Lawn"

Following the "Law"

Becoming a "Lawyer"

Taking a "Laxative"

Being a "Leader"

"Learning"

"Listening" to the "Lecture"

Keeping a "Ledger"

"Lending" a helping hand...

"Looking" through the "Lens"
(Enables us to see what is ahead)

Writing a "Letter"

Keeping both ends "Level"

Building a "Levee"

Pulling the "Lever"

"Liability" Insurance...

A trip to the "Library"

Getting your "License"

"Life" Insurance...

Seeing the "Light"!

Turning off the "Lights"

Reading the fine "Line"

The "Line" of credit...

Changing the "Linen"

Laying the "Linoleum"

Drinking enough "Liquids"

"Liquidating" your assets...

Making a "List", checking it twice...

Picking up all the "Litter"

Getting a "Loan"

Knowing the "Location"

"Locking" the door...
(Thou shall not steal; the punishments will become stronger)

Finding the right "Locker"

Settling into the "Lodge" for the night...

Cutting down the "Log"

Using "Logic"

Learning the "Logistics" of it all...

"Looking" both ways before crossing the street...

Seeing the "Loop-hole"

Collecting all the "Loot"

Finding the LORD!

Hitting the "Lottery"

Finding true "Love"

Being "Loyal"

Applying the "Lubricant"

Tightening the "Lug" nuts...

Hauling the "Lumber"

Fixing "Lunch"

Reading the "Lyrics"

Can you begin to see the pattern here?
I have "Learned" much through the gift given to me by our Lord and Savior!

****

**"He will also go before Him in the spirit and power of Elijah,
to turn the hearts of the father to the children,
and the disobedient to the wisdom of the just,
to make ready a people prepared for the Lord"**

LUKE 1:17

REWARDS OF THE LETTER "L"

"Labor-day"

"Lacking" nothing...

The "Lady-finger"

Seeing a "Lady-bug"

Being "Lady-like"

A swim in the "Lake"

"THE Lamb Of God"!

Owning "Land"

Our "Language"

"Lasagna"

The ability to "Last"

Getting in the "Last" word...

Laud:
To give praise or express devotion to; glorify.

"Laughter" is the best medicine...

"Lavish" Him

"Lead" by example...

The ability to turn over a new "Leaf"

"Leap" into action...

"Learn" while you still can...

Having two "Legs"

Having a "Leg" up on the competition...

The "Legacy" we leave behind...

Becoming a "Legend"

This is "Legitimate"

Leisure:
Freedom from time-consuming duties; having free time.

Lesson:
An experience or observation that imparts new knowledge or wisdom.

Understanding the "Letters"

Being "Level-headed"

"Liberty" and justice for all...

Might going to the "Library" be a form of reward?

"Life" itself is a reward...

Having the "Life-jacket" when you need it...

The ability to "Lift" the spirits of others...

He can "Lighten" the load...

Being well "Liked"

Made in His "Likeness"

Lilly-white:
Beyond reproach; blameless; pure.

"Lima-beans"? ☺

Might having all our "Limbs" be a form of reward?

"Lemon" or "Lime"

Knowing your "Limits"

The ability to stay out of the "Line" of fire...

A good "Line-up"

"Linguini"

Being the strong "Link"

Lionhearted:

A person resembling a lion, as in bravery or ferocity; courageous.

Soft "Lips"

The ability to "Listen" is a reward...

Good "Literature"

"Living" freely...

Make a "Life-long" commitment to Him!

Feeling "Lively" today...

"Living" for the moment of His return...

A full "Load"

A "Loaf" of bread; give when you can...

"Lobster" for me...

Having your picture in her "Locket"

Being "Logical" is also a reward...

A good "Logo"

A "Lollipop"

The "Lombardi" award...

"Longevity"

The ability to "Look" beyond...

The "Lord" Jesus Christ is our greatest reward!

Having a "Lot"

Looking "Lovely" today...

Finding true "Love"

"Loyalty"

Are you feeling "Lucky"?

A soothing "Lullaby"

A Fishing "Lure" that works...

It looks "Luscious"

There are many Rewards still left for you,
"Look" through the dictionary with your "loved" ones.

The line of "Life" with all below'
the "Lord" or "Lucifer" which way to go?
Tough "Love" at the start' though close to the heart,
This definition will not part.
"Listen" and "Learn" make a "List" today
Life made simpler' with this hurray!

****

"No one, when he has lit a lamp, covers it
with a vessel or puts *it* under a bed,
but sets *it* on a lampstand, that those who enter may see the light.
"For nothing is secret that will not be revealed,
nor *anything* hidden that will not
be known and come to light.

LUKE 8:16-17

PUNISHMENTS OF THE LETTER "L"

Forced "Labor"

Laceration:
To distress deeply; torn; mangled.

Lacking:
To be entirely without or having very little of: To need.

"Lackluster"

Laden:
Weighed down with a load; heavy; oppressed; burdened.

"Lagging" behind...

"Lame"

Watch out for the "Land-slide"

"Languishing" in your own sorrows...

A "Lapse" in memory...

A victim of "Larceny"

"Laryngitis"

Twenty "Lashes"

"Last" place...

Are you always "Late"?

"Later" than usual...

Law-less:
Unrestrained by law; disobedient.

Lax:
Showing little concern; remiss; negligent.

Being "Laid-off"

Do not be so "Lazy"

Fix the "Leak", follow the Commandments!

Stuck on a "Leash"

"Last" and "Least"

Are you still a little "Leery"?

Do not be "Left" behind...

"Leprosy"

Lethal:
Sufficient to cause or capable of causing death.

Do not be such a "Let-down"

Felling a little "Lethargic"?

Lewd:
Lustful; obscene; wicked.

You are "Liable" for your actions...

"Life-less"

"Light-headed"

Do not take Him "Lightly"

Struck by "Lightning"

Limbo:
The abode of souls kept from Heaven through
circumstance, such as lack of baptism.

Heaven is "off-limits" to those without belief!

Being a "Limp" dick...

Caught in the "Line" of fire...

Quit "Lingering", do it now!

Do not be the weak "Link"

157

Might being born with a "Lisp" be a punishment
passed down to the next generation?

List-less:
Marked by a lack of energy or enthusiasm; disinclined to any effort.

Stop all the "Littering"

He is "Livid" about now...

"Locked-out" of your own home...

The swarm of "Locusts"

No "Loitering"

Feeling "Lonely"

"Longing" for more...

Root for the "Long-shot"

"Long-suffering"

"Look-out" below...

Do you think I am "Loony"?

He will not "Lose"!

"Loss" of life...

Are you still "Lost"?

Try listening to the "Loud-mouth"

How "Low" Can you go,
"Lower" than you think?

Where is "Lucifer"?

Your "Luck" will run out...

It is hotter than "Luke-warm"

The "Lump" in your throat...

"Lust" is a Sin; Stop chasing after that which is already married!

Refrain from the "Lying"

The "Lynch-mob"

*By Understanding the "letters" We can see more
clearly what our "Lord" has in store!*

****

"But take heed to yourselves,
lest your hearts be weighed down with carousing,
drunkenness, and cares of this life, and that
Day come on you unexpectedly.
"For it will come as a snare on all those who
dwell on the face of the whole earth.
"Watch therefore, and pray always that you may
counted worthy to escape all these things that will come
to pass, and to stand before the Son of Man."

LUKE 21:34-36

"But when you see Jerusalem surrounded by armies,
then know that its desolation is near.
"Then let those who are in Judea flee to the mountains,
let those who are in the midst of her depart,
and let not those who are in the country enter her.
"For these are the days of vengeance,
that all things which are written may be fulfilled.
"But woe to those who are pregnant
and to those who are nursing babies in those days!
For there will be great distress in the land
and wrath upon this people.
"And they will fall by the edge of the sword,
and be led away captive into all nations.
And Jerusalem will be trampled by Gentiles
until the time of the Gentiles are fulfilled.

LUKE 21:20-24

ALL ABOUT THE LETTER "L"

Might you be a "Lawyer" "Loan officer" or "Librarian"?

"Let" your children know about the sacrifice of Jesus Christ!

"Look" towards the future...

"Learn" while there is still time...

"Lest" you be terrified...

The "Language" and the "Letters" equal "Love"

There is but "Little" time "Left"

Your "Luck" will run out...

The "Luxuries" are for the greedy...
(X marks the spot)

Be a "Luminary"

"Love" thy neighbor...

"Live" and let "Live"

Do not "Lounge" around, spread the word...

The "Lord" and "Lucifer" both begin with the capitol "L",
Which path do you wish upon your children?

Serve up some "Lemonade" and teach them...

The Second Coming does "Loom" close; also rhymes with the word doom!

"Loan" someone a helping hand...

"Lead" by example...

"Like" it or not here He comes...

LORD GOD of HOSTS

MAN IN THE MIDDLE

MAGNIFICENT

MAGICAL   MOUNTAINS

M

*"**Man**" starts with the letter "M"*
(The thirteenth of twenty-six letters, there we are again, "Man" in the middle).

Mans World, lots of ups and downs...

Middle   Mediocre   Midway

Murder   Mayhem

Lots of ups and downs in "Mans" world!

Might the time be near...

Maybe it has already begun...

Make the transformation...

Missing out...

Magical is the power of the Alphabet...

Meditate on it...

****

Hear, all you peoples!
Listen, O earth, and all that is in it!
Let the Lord God be a witness against you,
The Lord from His holy temple.
For behold, the Lord is coming out of His place;
He will come down And tread on the high places of earth.
The mountains will melt under Him,
And the valleys will split
Like wax before the fire,
Like waters poured down a steep place.

MICAH 1:2-4

You who are named the house of Jacob:

"Is the Spirit of the Lord restricted?
Are these His doings?
Do not My words do good
To him who walks uprightly?

MICAH 2:7

****

Man in the middle' with this He did fiddle'
The thirteenth of twenty-six,
This letter was His pick'
Oh what a trick!
Remember the ups and downs'
"Mediocrity" is the way it sounds
"Money" is "Mans World";
Greed leads to where satin was hurled.

COMMONALITY OF THE LETTER "M"

"Mans World"; In the "Middle"

That is the definition;
Will all our common "M" words give us an example
of what Mans world Evolves Around?

(Remember the ups and downs)...

Divide By three...

Commonality, Rewards, and Punishments...

"Money" begins with the letter "M"

****

"Whatever I tell you in the dark, speak in the light;
and what you hear in the ear, preach on the housetops.
"And do not fear those who kill the body but cannot kill the soul.
But rather fear Him who is able to destroy
both soul and body in hell.

MATTHEW 10:27-28

"Do not think that I came to bring peace on earth.
I did not come to bring peace but a sword.
"For I have come to
'set a man against his father, a daughter against her mother,
and a daughter-in-law against her mother-in-law';
"and 'a man's enemies will be those of his own household.'
"He who loves father or mother more than Me is not worthy of Me.
And he who loves son or daughter more
than Me is not worthy of Me.
"And he who does not take his cross and
follow after Me is not worthy of Me.
"He who finds his life will lose it, and he who
loses life for My sake will find it.

MATTHEW 10:34-39

The "Machine" fits well in "Mans World"
(Lots of ups and downs with them however)

"Made" in the USA...

The "Made-up" version...

The "Magazine" does well...

The "Magistrate"

"Magma" produces lots of ups and downs...

The "Magnet"

The "Magnifying" glass...

Having a "Maid"

The US "Mail"

"Majority" rules...

Do you wear too much "Make-up"?
(Sells very well in our world)

Being born a "Male"

How about the shopping "Mall"

Being the "Manager" bodes well...

The "Man-hole" takes us through lots of ups and downs...

As does reaching "Man-hood"

Check out the definition of the word "Manifold"

The "Mantle" over the fireplace...

"Manual" labor...

The "Manufacturer" and the "Manufacturing" plant seem to do quite well...

The "Manuscript" you are reading...

All the "Maps"

The word "Marginal" falls under "Mediocre"

Does the "Marijuana" and the "Meth" do well in "Mans World"?
(Or does it simply give us lots of ups and downs)

Being a "Marine" and going to the "Market"

"Marriage" fits well in "Mans World"
(It does however include the double "RR")

The "Mascot"

"Mass-transit"
(The double "SS")

The "Massage" fits well in our world, might it also be a reward?

All the different "Materials"

"Mathematics"
(Have we been to Engrossed in the Numbers that we failed to see the letters)?

A firm "Mattress"
(Can you understand the double "TT" in this word or the double "SS")?

Reaching "Maturity"

I'm going to "Maui"

The "Mayor", "Measurements" and the "Meat"

The "Mechanics" of it all...

How well do all the "Medicines" do?

Medium:
Something occupying a position or having a
condition midway between extremes.

Becoming a "Member" has its ups and downs...

The "Memorial" service...

Who's on the "Menu" for today?

The "Mercedes" does well in "Mans World"

Meridian:
Either half of such a great circle lying between the poles.

The "Myth" of the "Mermaid"

The "Message" you just received...

I am just the "Messenger"

"Metal"

All the "Metaphors"

Let's go to "Mexico"

Mezzanine:
A partial story occurring between two main stories of a building.

How about "Miami" instead...

Mid:
Being the part in the middle or center.

Middle:
Equally distant from the extremes or limits; central.

Midst:
The middle position or part; center.

Mid-way:
The middle of a way or distance; halfway.

Joining the "Military" gives us ups and downs
and it fits well into our world...

Run of the "Mill"

Our "Minds"

All the "Minerals"

"Mining" has lots of ups and downs...

The "Minister" at the local church?
Or might he have been rewarded with a better understanding?

Are their lots of ups and downs being a "Minor"?

Looking in the "Mirror"

The "Model"

Moderate:
Of medium or average quantity; quality, or extent; mediocre.

Your computer "Monitor"

The "Monkey"

The "Monologue"

The game of "Monopoly"

"Montana" is a beautiful place to visit...

As is "Monterey" California...

Check out the "Monument"

Traveling to the "Moon"

"Morphine" has its ups and downs...

The "Mosquito" is doing well in our world...

Being a "Mother" fits well, do we get ups and downs?

The "Motor" is our world...

The "Mountains" give us lots of ups and downs...

The "Movies" seem to do well...

"Multiplication" and "Multiply", there is that "Math" thing again...

"Muscles" and the "Music" we listen to...

Pass the "Mustard" and the "Mayo"

"Mutual" funds...

"Mystery" and "Mythology"

Ask yourself why are there so many "Muslims" in this world?
Might it be due to the fact that the word "Muslim"
begins and ends with the letter "M"?

"McDonalds", "Microsoft" and the "MGM
Grand" seem to do well in our world!
How many other "M" letter companies can you think of that are doing well?

Make no Mistake about it "Mankind" sits in
the Middle between Good and evil!

Which path will you take next?

****

Then He opened His mouth and taught them, saying;
Blessed *are* the poor in spirit,
For theirs is the kingdom of heaven.
Blessed *are* those who mourn,
For they shall be comforted.
Blessed *are* the meek,
For they shall inherit the earth.
Blessed *are* those who hunger and thirst for righteousness,
For they shall be filled.
Blessed *are* the merciful,
For they shall obtain mercy.
Blessed *are* the pure in heart,
For they shall see God.
Blessed *are* the peacemakers,
For they shall be called sons of God.
Blessed are those who are persecuted for righteousness' sake,
For theirs is the kingdom of heaven.

MATTHEW 5:2-10

REWARDS OF THE LETTER "M"

"M & M's

How about the "Macadamia" nut...
("Food" sure seems like it is a form of reward)

The "Macaroni"

Having been "Made" by God was a reward...

A good "Magazine"

"Magical" has a nice ring to it...

Magnanimous:
Noble of mind and heart; generous in forgiving; unselfish; gracious.

A "Magnetic" personality...

Magnificence:
Grand or imposing to the mind; marked by nobility of thought or deed.

The "Magnolia" is a nice flower...

The "Mahogany" floors...
(Where does greed start)?

Going to the "Mall", does it do well in our world?

The ability to "Maintain" your composure...

"Majestic" sounds like a nice reward!

Playing in the "Major League"?

The ability to "Make" sense...

"Make-believe"

A chocolate "Malt" please...

Being a "Man" is its own reward...

The ability to "Manage"

Belief is "Mandatory"

All "Mankind" has been rewarded;
Is the time for many just about up?

The ability to "Maneuver" out of the way...

The "Mango" sounds sweet...

He will be "Manifested" soon...

Good "Manners"

Saving "Many"

Winning the "Marathon"

"Marching" to the right beat...

A good "Marinade"

"Mark" these words...

The "Marquise" diamond...

Getting "Married"

A roasted "Marshmallow"

"Marvel" at His power...

He is "Marvelous"

"Mary" the mother of "Jesus Christ"

"Masculinity"

Being part of the "Mass" of believers...

Masterful:
Fit to command; vigorous; powerful.

He is the "Mastermind" behind it all...

"Match" Him if you can...

Finding your "Mate"

He will "Materialize" again...

"Maternal" instincts...

"Maternity":
(Now is not the time)

Enjoy the "Matinee" instead...

"Matrimony" is a form of reward...

You do "Matter"

"Matthew" and "Mark"!

Being "Mature"

"Maximize" His efforts...

Finding the end to the "Maze"

A lush "Meadow" to play in...

A good "Meal"

Meaningful:
Having meaning, function or purpose; significant.

The ability to "Measure" up...

Nice "Measurements"

"Meatloaf"

Winning a "Medal" is a form of reward...

The "Medal of Honor"

A good "Medley"

The "Meek" shall inherit the earth...

The ability to "Mellow-out"

A soft "Melody"

"Melts" in your mouth...

Memorable:
Worth being remembered or noted; remarkable.

"Memorial" Day

A good "Memory"

The ability to "Mend" your ways...

Being "Mentioned" in the book of life...

Lord have "Mercy" on us...

"Merge" with Him...

The Alphabet does have "Merit"

Merry:
Full of high-spirited gaiety; jolly.

The ability to "Mesmerize" those around you...

Send the "Message"!

Become a "Messenger"!

The "Messiah" Was Our Greatest Reward!

He is "Methodical" and "Meticulous"

Having the "Midas" touch...

How "Mighty" is He!

The next "Millennium"
(The thousand-year reign)!

Becoming a "Millionaire";
Give to those less fortunate; earn a place in heaven!

The "Mind" is a wonderful thing...

"Mingle" with Him...

"Minimize" the damage...

Become a "Minister"

The "Mink" coat;
How much is enough?

A Chocolate "Mint"

Seeing a "Miracle"

A fine "Mist"

Getting caught under the "Mistletoe"

Being "Mobile"

A Double "Mocha"

Living "Modestly"

Become a good "Mold"

Seize the "Moment"

Having "Money" can be a Reward, if it is used the right way!

Being in a good "Mood" is its own reward...

High "Morals"

Waking each "Morning"

A loving "Mother"

Having the "Motivation" it takes...

Taking a trip to the "Mountains"

The ability to "Multiply"

"Multiple" orgasms...

Enjoy the "Music"

Travel to the "Museum"

The ability to "Muster" those around you...

"Mutual" love...

Solving the "Mystery"

A certain "Mystique"

*A "Myriad" of Rewards awaits those that chose
to follow in the path of Righteousness!*

*There are many "Rewards" for mankind we must
however make more of an effort.*

****

**"Enter by the narrow gate; for wide *is* the gate and broad *is* the
way that leads to destruction, and there are many who go in by it.
"Because" narrow *is* the gate and difficult
is the way which leads to life,
and there are few who find it.**

MATTHEW 7:13-14

*Might the End-times "Gate" be that of following and learning
more about our "LANGUAGE" & "LETTERS"?*

The letters will lead us to the House of Jacob!

*****

The "Lost Books of the Bible" is supposedly a
collection of stories and scripture that
The Early leaders of the Church did not feel were
worthy of being added to the Bible.
The following text comes from the last pages of this book.

THE TESTAMENT OF BENJAMIN
(The Twelfth Son of Jacob and Rachel)

And the twelve tribes shall be gathered together there,
And all the Gentiles,
until the Most High shall send forth His salvation
in the visitation of an only-begotten prophet.

(Chapter II, Verse 6)

And there shall arise in the latter days one beloved of the Lord,
Of the tribe of Judah and Levi,
A doer of His good pleasure in his mouth,
With new knowledge enlightening the Gentiles.

(Chapter II, Verse 26)

And he shall be inscribed in the holy books,
both his work and his word,
And he shall be a chosen one of God forever.

(Chapter II, Verse 28)

The "Punishments" that will soon fall upon mankind
If we do not change our course are listed next.
Are you prepared to deal with them?

Unfortunately I believe that we will not do what is needed, thus...

THE PUNISHMENTS...

PUNISHMENTS OF THE LETTER "M"

The "Machete"

The "Machine Gun"

Going "Mad"

Madness:
Insanity; lunacy.

Maelstrom:
A whirlpool of extraordinary size or violence.

Magma:
The molten matter under the Earth's crust.

Dealing with the whole "Magnitude" of it all...

"Maggots"

Malady:
A disease, disorder, or ailment.

"Malaria", "Mal-formed", "Mal-functioning", "Malice" and "Malicious"

"Maligned", "Malignancy", "Malnourished",
"Malodorous" and "Malpractice"

Are just a few...

Mange:
A contagious skin disease caused by parasitic mites.

Mangled:
To mutilate or disfigure by battering, hacking, tearing, or cutting.

Dealing with the "Maniac"

Being "Manipulated"

Bad "Manners"

"Man-eater" and "Man-slayer"

These are a few more of those punishments that sit around the corner...

"Marked"

"Marooned"

"Marshall Law"

"Mass" Execution...

"Massacred"

"Materialism"

"Mauled"

"Mayhem"

"Meager"

Being "Mean"

"Measles"
(Try not to pass them on)

Unable to "Measure-up"

"Meddling" in others affairs...

Needing a "Medic"

"Mediocrity"

Melee:
The confused hand-to-hand fighting; a violent free-for-all.

Becoming a "Menace" to society...

Mendacious:
Lying; untruthful; false.

"Menopause"

Merciless:
Having no mercy; pitiless; cruel.

Mess:
A cluttered, untidy, usually dirty state or condition.

The "Meteor" shower...

"Microscopic" disease...

Stuck in the "Middle"

When the clock strikes "Midnight"

Miffed:
A petulant, bad-tempered mood; easily offended.

The "Migraine"

Mindless:
Lacking intelligence or good sense; foolish.

Being part of the "Minority"

There are many, many punishments beginning with the "MIS-"
Do not "Miss" them; look for yourselves all that awaits "Mankind"!

"Missing" in action...

"Mistaking" His power...

Being "Mistreated" and "Misunderstood" are just a few...

Are you feeling a little "Mixed-up" about now?

How many of these punishments have we already experienced?

Moan:
A low, sustained, mournful sound, usually indicative of sorrow or pain.

Mob:
A large, disorderly crowd regarded as disorderly or ignorant.

Being "Mocked"

Is "Modesty" a punishment?

Moil:
To toil or slave; drudgery.

It's "Molded"

"Molten" lava...

"Money" is the root of all evil!

"Mono"

"Monotonous"

"Monthly"

The "Moocher"
(No one should have to be; give)

In a bad "Mood"

"Morbid"

Wanting "More"

Visiting the "Morgue"

...In the "Morning"

He does have a "Motive"

"Mourning" for those who are lost...

Stuck in the "Muck"

Just plain "Mud"

Do not "Muffle" His word...

An ugly "Mug"
(Might this be a punishment handed down)?

The "Mug-shot"

"Mull" over it...

The "Mumbling" has already started...

Mumbo-jumbo:
Confusing or meaningless activity; incantation.

"Multiple" gun shot wounds...

A "Multitude" of punishments await...

Becoming a "Mummy"

Getting the "Mumps"
(Try not to pass it to the next generation)

The "Munsters"
(Trying to maintain a sense of humor here)

Mundane:
Typical of or concerned with the ordinary.

Murder:
Homicide; manslaughter; an unlawful killing.

Are things a little "Murky" for you?

Murphy's Law:
If anything can go wrong it will.

Might "Muscular Dystrophy" have been passed down?

Turned to "Mush"

The "Mushroom" Cloud...

Muss:
To make messy or untidy; rumpled, a state of disorder.

You "Must" believe...

"Mutation"

"Munch-kin"

"Mute"

Mutinous:
Rebellious; disaffected; turbulent and uncontrollable.

"Muzzled"

"Many" Are the Ways of our Punishments...

****

But when you hear of wars and rumors of wars,
do not be troubled;
for such things must happen,
but the end is not yet.
For nation will rise against nation,
and kingdom against kingdom.
And there will be earthquakes in various places,
and there will be famines and troubles.
These are the beginnings of sorrows.

MARK 13:7-8

ALL ABOUT THE LETTER "M"

"Might" you be a "Mail-man" or a "Mortician"?
"Maybe" you are in the "Medical" field,
Or are you a "Math" professor?

Do you have "Mixed" feelings?

"Make" no "Mistake" about it;
The end times are near, unless we can change...
Being in the "Middle" gives us a chance...

Do you like the "Motorcycle"?

"Mayonnaise" or "Mustard"?

Do not think this is "Make-believe"
The "Mind" is a terrible thing to waist!

"Might" the time have already begun...

"Misery" loves company...

Do you smoke the "Marlboro" brand or just the "Marijuana"?
"Might" it be both?

"Meat" and "Mashed" Potatoes...

Lord have "Mercy" on us...

"Make" the Change to His Side...

****

"For which is easier to say,
'Your sins are forgiven you,' or to say, 'Arise and walk'?
"But that you may know that the Son of Man
has power on earth to forgive sins" -
then He said to the paralytic,
"Arise, take up your bed, and go to your house."
And he arose and departed to his house.
Now when the multitudes saw it, they marveled and glorified God,
who had given such power to men.

MATTHEW 9:5-8

Notes

NEEDED

N

Needed but has Needs...

NOTHING

"Need," I say more...

Now is the time...

Not tomorrow...

Nobody is exempt...

No one...

None...

Next...

You are Necessary...

Our days are Numbered...

Nestle by the fire and accept Jesus Christ as your savior...

Nice to know you...

****

"And to the angel of the church in Philadelphia write,
"These things says He who is holy, He who is
true, "He who has the key of David,
He who opens and no one shuts, and shuts and no one opens".
"I know your works, See, I have set before you
an open door, and no one can shut it,
for you have a little strength, have kept My
word, and have not denied My name.
"Indeed I will make those of the synagogue of Satan,
who say they are Jews and are not, but lie-indeed I will
make them come and worship before your feet,
and to know that I have loved you.
"Because you have kept My command to preserve, I also
will keep you from the hour of trial which shall come upon
the whole world, to test those who dwell on earth.
"Behold, I am coming quickly!
Hold fast what you have, that no one may take your crown.
"He who overcomes, I will make him a pillar in the temple of
My God, and he shall go out no more. I will write on him the
name of My God and the name of the city of My God, the New
Jerusalem, which comes down out of heaven from My God.
And I will write on him My new name.
"He who has an ear, let him hear what
the Spirit says to the churches."

REVELATION 3:7-13

COMMONALITY OF THE LETTER "N"

Needed but, has Needs of its' own!

Each "Common" Word in our English Language
beginning with the letter "N"
Gives this to us...

How many of the Rewards and Punishments do you know?

"Nurture" your belief...

****

And all the people went their way to eat and drink,
To send portions and rejoice greatly,
Because they understood the words that were declared to them.

NEHEMIAH 8:12

Those with the Dominate "N"
You are "Needed"

"Now" is the time to grab the Dictionary,
Read with your loved ones all those common "N" words that you know...

****

The LORD *is* good,
A stronghold in the day of trouble;
And He knows those who trust in Him.

NAHUM 1:7

"Needed" with "Needs" Even "Nature" has seeds' Are you "Naive"?
"None" are exempt'
For the words "Woman" and "Man"
Include the letter "N" And so does the "Name" Dan!

The "Nail" is "needed" to hold things together, does it "need" the hammer...

Your "Name" is "Needed", what are your "Needs"?

The "Nanny" needs direction

Taking a "Nap"

The "Napkin" needs to be used...

"Narcotics" need supervision...

The "Nark"
(The letter "K" represents deceit)

Narrative:
Consisting of or characterized by the telling of a story.
(Tell His story)

Our "Nasal" passages need a clear path...

Our "Nation" needs to follow the ten...

The "Native"

"NATO" & "NASA"

"Natural" gas...

"Nature" needs to be protected...

The "Navigator" needs the compass...

The "Navy" needs the Marines...

The "Nazarene" needs your faith...

The "Needle" needs the thread...

"Negative" feedback is needed...

The "Negligee" needs discretion...

The ability to "Negotiate" is also needed...

The "Negro" and the "Neighbor" both seem to
have needs, are they not needed!

The "Neon" lights...

Give to your "Nephew"

Nepotism:
Favoritism shown or patronage granted by persons in high office
to relatives or close friends. (Needs the "common" people)

The planet "Neptune"

Our "Nerves"

The "Nest" is needed to protect the young...

The "Networks" are needed, what might those needs be?

The "Newlyweds" have many needs...

The "News" needs to be unbiased...

The "New Testament" needs to be read!

Just a "Nibble" is all that is needed...

The "Niece" has her needs too...

The middle of the "Night" needs caution...

The "Nile" river needs water...

"Nitrogen" and the "Noise"

The "Nomad" needs a home...

The "Nomination" needs your vote...

"Non-fiction" needs your attention...

There are a lot of words beginning with "North" that fit this definition...

"Nostradamus" needs to be taken seriously...

The "Notary"

The "Notebook"

The "Nouns" need the pro-nouns...

"Nourishment" is needed...

The "Novel" needs to be read...

The "Nozzle" is no good without the gas or liquid...

"Nuclear" energy needs caution...

The "Numbers" are needed, the "Nun" too...

The "Nuptials" need to be taken seriously...

The "Nurse" needs the Doctor...

The "Nut" needs the shell...

Good "Nutrition" still needs exercise...

The "Nymphomaniac" needs sex...

All these things are needed yet have needs of their own in some form or another.

There are more in the dictionary still left for you...

****

**Then the LORD said to Moses:
"How long will these people reject Me?
And how long will they not believe Me,
with all the signs which I have performed among them?**

NUMBERS 14:11

NOW IS THE TIME

High in the Clouds a Map of our Nation I did see,
Not once but twice with one day between' could it really be?
The Northeast is where I looked first'
this where a fire did burst,
The State of Florida was next in line'
little islands were all I could find.
As my eyes began to roam'
looking for the Houston Astrodome;
All I saw was lake and foam.
To the West my eyes did veer'
The Coastline gone', as we fear!
The Northwest is where I call home'
The Mountains there had blown their dome.
Towards the Rockies is where Thine eyes then went,
Behold for this' a Place to Repent!

****

Neither our kings or our princes,
Our priests nor our fathers,
Have kept Your law,
Nor heeded Your commandments and Your testimonies,
With which You testified against them.
For they have not served You in their kingdom,
Or in the many good *things* that you gave them,
Or in the large and rich land which You set before them;
Nor did they turn from their wicked works.

NEHEMIAH 9:34-35

REWARDS OF THE LETTER "N"

Hitting the "Nail" on the head...

The ability to run around "Naked", was this lost because of sin?

A strong "Name"

The ability to get a good "Nap" when you need it...

"Narrow" is the path...

A strong "Nation"

Our "National" parks...

"Natural" ability...

"Nature" gives us many rewards...

The ability to "Navigate" through the tough times...

"Navy" beans...

The "Nazarene" is our most precious reward!

Having Him "Nearby" will be a reward for us all...

Being "Neat" and orderly...

Being "Necessary"

Nectar:
The drink of the Gods: Any delicious or invigorating drink.

Having your "Needs" fulfilled...

Finding the "Needle" in the haystack...

The ability to "Negotiate" Your way into heaven...

Good "Neighbors"

The "Nephew" and the "Niece"

"Nerves" of steel...

The "Nest-egg"
(Give if you can)

Becoming a "New" believer...

The "New Testaments"

Being "Next" in line...

"Niagara Falls"

Being "Nice" is its' own reward...

Praying "Nightly" will entitle you to many rewards...

Nimble:
Quick and agile in movement or action; cleverly alert.

Nirvana:
The state of absolute blessedness; freedom from the external world.

"Nobility"

Getting the "Nod"

Will you be "Nominated"?

Non-paralleled:
Without rival; matchless; unequaled.

Working "Non-stop"

"Non-violent"

"Noodles"

Being considered "Normal"?

A visitor from the "North-pole"
(Try to smile)

"Notable"

A "Notch" above...

Being "Noticed" gives us many rewards...

Giving "Nourishment" to those in need...

The ability to do it "Now"

The ability to "Nudge" others into action...

A golden "Nugget"

The "Numbers" led us to DNA...

"Nurture" your beliefs...

"Nutmeg"

In a "Nut-shell":

How much more proof do you "Need"?

****

The LORD *is* slow to anger and great in power,
And will not at all acquit *the wicked*.
The LORD has His way
In the whirlwind and in the storm,
And the clouds are dust of His feet.

NAHUM 1:3

****

He who scatters has come before your face.
Man the fort!
Watch the road!
Strengthen *your* flanks!
Fortify *your* power mightily.

NAHUM 2:1

PUNISHMENTS OF THE LETTER "N"

Being "Nabbed"

Nag:
To pester or annoy by constant scolding, complaining
or urging; to find fault constantly.

Naive:
Lacking critical ability or analytical insight; not subtle or ingenious.

Nameless:
Unknown by name; obscure.

Having only a "Nanosecond" before He comes for you...

Narcissism:
Excessive admiration of oneself.

Becoming addicted to the "Narcotics"

"Narrow" minded...

Nasty:
Disgusting to see, smell or touch; filthy; foul; indecent.

Naughty:
Disobedient; mischievous; perverse; wicked; evil

Are you feeling "Nauseated"?

Saying "Nay" to those in need...

Where the "Nazi's" a form of punishment?

Neanderthal:
A crude, boorish, or old-fashioned person

The time is "Near"

"Necrophilia"

A "Negative" personality is a form of punishment...

As is feeling "Neglected"

Your "Nemesis" is another...

Are your "Nerves" shot or are you just a little "Nervous"?

"Neurosis", "Neurotic", Neutered" and "Neutralized"

The "Neutron" and the "Nuclear" bomb...

"Never" being saved...

Getting just a "Nibble"

"Nicked" by the sword...

Addicted to "Nicotine"

This is more than a "Nightmare"

"Nip" it in the bud...

"Nitrogen dioxide"

Nitwit:
A stupid or silly person.

Saying "No" to those in need...

Being a "Nobody"

There are many punishments beginning with "Non-",
Look them up with a loved one.

Strung-up by a "Noose"

The "Nose-bleed"

Stop being a "Nuisance" to others...

He can "Nullify" our very existence!

Are you feeling a little "Numb"?

Are you just plain "Nuts"?

"Needless" to say the Punishments can be severe,
Save your soul. Do the Best you Can!

He can see when we are trying to do better...

****

Who can stand before His indignation?
And who can endure the fierceness of His anger?
His fury is poured out like fire,
And the rocks are thrown down by Him.

NAHUM 1:6

"Behold I am against you," says the LORD of hosts,
"I will burn your chariots in smoke,
and the sword shall devour your young lions;
I will cut off your prey from the earth,
and the voice of your messengers shall be heard no more."

NAHUM 2:13

Therefore I will look to the LORD;
I will wait for the God of my salvation;
My God will hear me.

NAHUM 7:7

ALL ABOUT THE LETTER "N"

Are you a "Night-watchman" or a "Naturalist"?

Might you be a "Nurse" or a "Nanny"?

You are "Needed"

Have you "Noticed" His power yet?

Try doing something "Nice" for someone you do "Not" know...

Have some "Neapolitan" Ice cream...

"Nestle" by the fire with your "Niece" and "Nephew"

"Nature" will take its course...

Try not to be to "Naive"

"Nachos"

How much of a "Nest-egg" do you have?

Head "North"

"Nothing" but belief can save you...

Do you enjoy reading the "News" or the paperback "Novel"?

Are you "Near-sighted"?

Might you be a little "Nocturnal"?

Try some "Needle-work"

Teach your "Next-of-kin"

Was "New Orleans" just a warning?

"Next" time it might be a lot worse...

"Null" and void...

OMEGA

ORBIT   **OCEAN**

OTHERS

O

(The circle of life complete)!

Completes life, especially for others...

Orgasm

OBSOLETE

Try not to be "Offended"

*O*pportunity awaits...

*O*pen the door to His world...

*O*therwise...

*O*bsolete...

*O*r will you be seen in heaven...

*O*nly He can save you...

*O*rder now...

****

Though you ascend *as* high as the eagle,
And though you set your nest among the stars,
From there I will bring you down," says the LORD.

OBADIAH 4

"But on Mount Zion there shall be deliverance,
And there shall be holiness;
The house of Jacob shall possess their possessions.

OBADIAH 17

*O*ut of this world...
*O*nly those that have "True Belief"

Tell *O*thers about the power of the Alphabet...
Tell *O*thers about the sacrifice of Jesus Christ...

****

Then saviors shall come to Mount Zion
To judge the mountains of Esau,
And the kingdom shall be the LORD'S.

OBADIAH 21

COMMONALITY OF THE LETTER "O"

Completes the cycle of life: Especially for "Others"

The letter "O" gives us all those things in our world that makes life more complete...

Tell "Others"

"Organize" those around you...

Otherwise you might be the Only One...

****

"For the day of the LORD upon all the nations is near;
As you have done, it shall be done to you;
Your reprisal shall return upon your own head.

OBADIAH 15

"Open" the door to His world...

The "Oak" tree provides us with all the paper products...

The "Oar" completes the life of the rowboat...

The "Oasis" gives life to the desert...

The "Oats" feed many...

Taking an "Oath" to the Lord completes life for all...

Your name in the "Obituaries" completes your life on earth...

"Observance" of the Sabbath day...

The "Observatory"

The "Obstetrician" and Your "Occupation"

The "Ocean" completes the cycle of life for millions...

The "Odors" we smell...

The "Offers" we receive and the "Offerings" we give to others...

Going to the "Office"

The "Officer" of the law...

The "Official" at the ballgame...

"Off-shore" drilling...

Our "Offspring"

"Oil"

Becoming "Old"

The "Old" Testament...

The "Omega"!
(The beginning and the end)

The "Operation" and the telephone "Operator"

Your "Opinion" and your "Opponent"

"Opposites" attract...

The "Optic" nerves...

The "Orbit"

The "Orchid"

Being "Ordained"

Law and "Order"

Our "Organs"

"Organization"

The "Oriental"

The "Orientation" you are now receiving...

The point of "Origin"

The "Orphanage"

The "Orthodox" religion...

"Others"

An "Ounce" of respect...

The Great "Outdoors"

The "Outfit" you are wearing...

Female "Ovaries"

"Ownership"

"Oxygen"

&

The "Ozone" layer!

The gift for "Others" includes our br'others
Where would we be without our m'others?
The "Ocean" gives life to so many' this We must not delete,
"Life so complete" we pray the "O" He shall make not "Obsolete"!

****

"Behold, happy *is* the man whom God corrects;
Therefore do not despise the chastening of the Almighty.
For He bruises, but He binds up;
He wounds, but His hands make whole.
He shall deliver you in six troubles,
Yes, in seven no evil shall touch you.
In famine He shall redeem you from death,
And in war from the power of the sword.
You shall be hidden from the scourge of the tongue,
And you shall not be afraid of destruction when it comes.
You shall laugh at destruction and famine,
And you shall not be afraid of the beasts of the earth.
For you shall have a covenant with the stones of the field,
And the beasts of the field shall be at peace with you.
You shall know that your tent *is* in peace;
You shall visit your dwelling and find nothing amiss.
You shall also know that your descendants *shall be* many,
And your offspring like the grass of the earth.
You shall come to the grave at a full age,
As a sheaf of grain ripens in its season.
Behold, this we have searched out;
It *is* true.
Hear it, and know for yourself."

JOB 5:17-27

REWARDS OF THE LETTER "O"

Finding the "Oasis" in the middle of the desert...

"Obedience"

The ability to "Obey" the Ten Commandments...

Realizing His "Objective"

Observable:
Deserving or worthy of notice or mention; noteworthy.

"Observant" enough to see His signs...

Find belief and "Observe" Him in action...

The ability to overcome the "Obstacles"

"Obtaining" the word...

Enjoying the special "Occasions"

"Occupying" a place in heaven...

Defying all the "Odds"

Being on the "Offensive"

Receiving His "Offer"

Make it "Official"

Having lots of "Offspring"

Doing it "Often"

I'm "OK"

Growing "Old"

"Old Glory"

Being "Old-School"

The "Old" Testament...

The "Olive" trees...

Becoming an "Olympiad"

The Alpha and the "Omega"

The "Omelet"

A good "Omen"

Being "On" the ball...

Having to be told only "Once"

"Onward" we shall go...

"Opening" your heart and your wallet...

"Open-minded"

"Operable"

Take the "Opportunity" and doing it now...

Defeating the "Opposition"

Optimism:
The belief that the universe is improving and
that good will triumph over evil.

"Optimize" your beliefs...

A glass of "Orange" juice...

Surviving the whole "Ordeal"

Remaining "Orderly"

Above the "Ordinary"

The ability to "Organize" your loved ones...

Knowing the "Origin" of this message...

"Originality"

The ability to be "Ourselves"

Knowing the "Outcome"

"Outdistancing" the pack...

"Outliving" the others...

"Outplaying" the opponent...

Receiving an "Outpouring" of affection...

Playing "Outside"

"Outstanding"

"Overcoming" all the odds...

Shift into "Overdrive"

"Overflowing" with compassion...

Not being "Overlooked"

"Owing" nothing...

Not being on your "Own"

"Oysters" on the half shell...

The letter "O" is all about the help for "Others" do your part and teach them of the Sacrifice of Jesus Christ. Tell "Others" about the Power of the Alphabet!

The door will Only be Open for a short time...

Or will you receive the Punishments?

PUNISHMENTS OF THE LETTER "O"

Oaf:
A stupid or clumsy person.

Lying under "Oath" will get you His punishments...

Obesity:
Might He be punishing our children for our sins?

"Objection" overruled...

"Obliterated", "Oblivious", "Obnoxious", "Obscene", and "Obscure"

"Obsolete", "Obtrusive", and "Obtuse"

Heaven being "Off-limits"

A bad "Omen"

Being "Omitted" from the book of life...

"One" is a lonely number...

Dealing with the impending "Onslaught"

It will be "Open" season...

Oppressed:
To weigh heavily upon, especially so as to depress the mind or spirits.

Ostracized:
To banish or exclude from a group; shut out; shunned.

"Ouch" it hurts doesn't it?

He is "Outraged" about now...

There are many punishments beginning with the
word "Out-" and the word "Over -"!

Look them up, they are on the way!

"Over -And - Out"

ONCE AND FOR ALL

By William E. Beavers

Our Lord above has prepared for me a special place,
As He rids the human race of many an unbelieving face.
How can He be so cruel you say'
Believe it's done with an Amazing grace.

Earthquakes, Tsunami's, Volcano's and War
All running at the same Spectacular pace.

Pestilence, Famine, and the Meteor Shower too,
Just in case...

Many a Christian Soul Are Heaven Sent
Many whose last words shall be "I Repent"
Disbeliever's, well we know where they went?

One nation "Under" God, we bent
His love which He lent' recedes with nary a scent.

Our money on the poor it was not spent
The "Tenth Commandment" is your hint...

This and the Doctrines of men shall cause our fall,

Follow the "Ten" Once and for All!

ALL ABOUT THE LETTER "O"

"Obstetrician", "Orthodontist", and those that write the "Obituaries"
(Can you see how these fall into the definition of the letter "O")?

Take an "Oath" with our Lord and Savior!

You are "Obligated"!

Are you somewhat "Obsessive"?

Do you enjoy the "Orchestra"?

Add some "Onion", or an "Olive" to the "Omelet's"

What's the special "Occasion"?

"Occasionally" is not good enough...

"Orchestrate" your family...

Read the "Old Testament", do it "Often"

"Oh" what a relief it is...

"Onward" we will go...

"Obsolete" is His punishment...

It "Only" takes "One" that believes to influence many "Others"

"Once" is not enough...

Law and "Order"

"Obey" the Ten Commandments!

Do not be caught "Off-Guard"!

"Open" the Door to His World...

****

**Then the four living creatures said, "Amen!"
And the twenty-four elders fell down and worshipped
Him who lives forever and ever.**

REVELATION 5:14

Notes

PERFECTION

PURPOSE

PLANET

PLAN

PEOPLE

P

(The line of life from top to bottom, all things good enclosed up top).

A More "Profound Purpose"

Purgatory

"Persist" in finding the truth

*P*erhaps you still need some more convincing?

*P*atience is a virtue...

*P*rotect your soul...

*P*roof is in the letters...

*P*lan on being fascinated...

*P*ersist in getting all the facts...

*P*ersonally, by understanding the power of the letters, there is no doubt...

*P*ray often...

*P*lease Him...

*P*ray often...

*P*lease Him...

*P*ray often...

*P*ass all His tests...

****

who are kept by the power of God through faith for
the salvation ready to be revealed in the last time.
In this you greatly rejoice, though now for a little while,
if need be,
you have been grieved by various trials,
that the genuineness of your faith,
being much more precious than gold that
perishes, though it is tested by fire,
may be found to praise, honor, and glory
at the revelation of Jesus Christ.

1 PETER 1:5-7

COMMONALITY OF THE LETTER "P"

A More "Profound Purpose"

*The letter "P" will give us those words in
our Language that serve a more;
"Powerful Purpose"*

Might this Include those "People" with the Dominate "P"?

"Punishments" have a "Purpose"

"Do Not" forget the "Rewards."

"Pray"

*Father:
We pray this day that you will take mercy on our souls.
Forgive each of us, for we All fall short of your glory,
And Enlighten us to Your special ways.
In the name of our Lord and Savior Jesus Christ.
Amen.*

*The "Pacemaker" seems to have a profound
purpose, as does the "Pacific" ocean...*

The "Package" you just received...

The "Paddle"

The "Padlock"

Each "Page"

Getting "Paid"

The "Pail" and the "Painter"

"Pajamas" and the "Palace"

The wooden "Pallet"

The "Palm" of your hand...

The "Pamphlet" you just read...

The frying "Pan" and the "Pants" you are wearing...

The "Paper" the "Paper-weight" and all the "Paper-work"

The "Pap" smear...

Making "Par" on the last hole...

The "Parables" in the bible...

What would happen without the "Parachute"?

The next "Paragraph"

The "Paramedic" the "Parameters" and all the "Paraphernalia"

"Parasites"

"Parcel post"

Our "Parents"

The "Parish" at the local church...

All the "Parks"

"Parliament" and the "Parlor"

The "Pass" through the mountains...

The "Passport" and our "Past"

The "Pastor" and the "Pasture"

The "Patent" and the "Paternity" test...

The "Path" trough the woods...

The "Patient" and the "Patriarch"

The "Patrol" ahead of you...

Seeing the "Pattern"

Reading the book of "Paul"

The "Pavement"

The "Pawn" shop...

The "Payroll"

"Peace"

The "Pearly" gates...

The "Peasant" serves a purpose, as does the "Pebble"

The foot "Pedal" and the "Pedestrian"

"Peeing"

"Peeling" the fruit...

The "Peep-hole"

The "Pen" and the "Pencil"

The "Penis" and the... (Vagina)

The "Penitentiary" serves a profound purpose...

A "Penny" for your thoughts...

Having a "Pension" to fall back on...

The word "People" has two "P's"

The "Pep" talks...

The "Perch" serves a purpose for the "Parrot"

"Perfume"

The "Perimeter"

Having your last "Period"

The "Periscope"

Having the right "Permits"

The books of "Peter"

The "Petition" you just signed...

"Petroleum"

The "Pharaoh"

"Pharmaceuticals"

Philanthropy:
The effort or inclination to increase the well being
of mankind, as by charitable aid.

The "Philosopher"

The "Phone" and the "Photocopier"

The "Photos" and the "Photographer"

The "Physician" and "Physics"

The "Picket" fence...

Taking "Pictures"

The "Pilgrims"

The "Pill"

The "Pillow", the "Pilot", and the safety "Pin"

The "Pioneer" and all the "Pipes"

The "Pitcher" in the game and the "Pitcher" that holds the water...

Having a "Plan" and all the "Plants"

The "Plane" and the "Planet"

"Plankton" and "Plasma"

"Plaster" and "Plastic"

The "Plate" the "Plateau" the "Platform" and the "Platinum"

The whole "Platoon"

"Playing"

The "Plaza" and the "Plea-bargain"

The "Pledge" of allegiance...

The "Plot" and the "Plow"

The "Plug" and the "Plumber"

"Pluto" and "Plutonium"

"Plywood" and your "Pockets"

The "Poem" the "Poet" and the "Poetry"

The "Poet" the "Painter" the "Police" and the "Pope"
The letter "P" gives us Hope,
A more "Profound Purpose" in this,
the "Punishments" you will not wish!
The "Planet" and all the "People"

"Pray" for this under the Steeple.

Poker:
(Includes the letter "K", is deceit present)?

The "Polar" ice caps and the "Politician"

The "Poll" booths...

"Pollination"

Being "Poor" and the entire "Population" has a significant purpose...

The "Porch" and the "Pork"

The "Porpoise" and the shipping "Port"

Your "Portfolio" and your "Portrait"

The fence "Post" and the "Post-office"

The "Postage-stamp" and the "Post-mark"

The "Pot" and the "Pouch"

"Poultry" and the "Power"

The "Power-play" and the "Pow-Wow"

221

"Prayer"

The power of the "PRE-"

The "Presents" and the "Press" are a few as is the "Preview"!

"The "Priest" has a commitment...

"Primary" Colors and the "Primer"

The "Prince" and the "Princess"

The "Principle" and the fine "Print"

The "Prize" and the "Proceeds"

The "Procedure" and the "Process"

The "Produce" and all the "Products"

The "Professor" and the "Program"

The "Project" you are working on...

The "Promissory" note and the "Prong"

The "Pronoun" and the "Proof"

"Propane" and the "Propeller"

"Property" and the "Prophet"

The "Proposal" and the "Proprietor"

The "Prosecutor" and the "Prostitute"

"Protein" and the "Protester"

The book of "Proverbs" provides...

The "PTA" and the "Publication" you are reading...

The "Publisher" and the "Pulpit"

The "Purse" and the ability to solve the "Puzzle"

How much of a "Profound Purpose" do we get from all these things?

*There are many more words still left, they all
do serve a more significant purpose.*

There are a "Pyramid" of punishments...

"Pray"

"Purify" Him

"Place" your trust in them...

"Peace" be with you and yours always...

****

**"Then they will call on me, but I will not answer;
They will seek me diligently, but they will not find me.
Because they hated knowledge
And did not choose the fear of the LORD,
They would have none of my counsel
And despised my every rebuke.**

PROVERBS 1:28-30

WILLIAM E. BEAVERS

REWARDS OF THE LETTER "P"

Working at your own "Pace"

Pacifism/Pacify:
The belief that disputes between nations should and can be settled peacefully.
(Includes the letter "F")

Paean:
A song of joyful praise or exultation; an expression of joy.

Winning the beauty "Pageant"

The ability to "Paint"

Being "Pampered"

"Pancakes"

The ability to not "Panic"

Shooting "Par"

Understanding the "Parables"

Enjoy the "Parade"

Paradise:
The Garden of Eden:
Heaven, the resting-place of righteous souls awaiting the Resurrection.

Receiving a "Pardon"

Our "Parents"

Parfait:
A dessert made of cream, eggs, and sugar.

"Parity"

A trip to the "Park"

Being a "Part" of the believers...

Having a "Partner"

Enjoy the "Party"

"Passing" all the test...

Receiving a "Passage" into heaven...

Passion:
Any powerful emotion such as love and joy: Boundless enthusiasm.

Being "Passionate" about Him...

Learning from your "Past"

"Pastries"

A "Pat" on the back...

Following the right "Path"

Patience:
The capacity of calm endurance; tolerant.

Patronage:
Support, encouragement, or championship from others.

Hitting "Pay-dirt"

"Peace"

"Peaches" and "Pears"

"Pecan Pie"

Getting a "Peek" at the future...

Penance:
A feeling of sorrow for wrongdoing or sin
prompting one to a firm amendment.

The ability to "Perceive" the truth...

"Perfection"

"Performing" His requirements...

A nice "Perfume"

Knowing His "Perimeters"

Being "Perky"

Having a "Permanent" place with Him...

Perpetual:
Lasting for eternity; unlimited duration.

Perseverance:
The holding of a course of action or belief without giving way; steadfastness.

"Persistence" in the truth...

A wonderful "Personality"

Having a true "Perspective"

The ability to "Persuade" others...

Owning a "Pet"

Phenomenal:
Extraordinary; outstanding; remarkable.

"Pickles" and the "Picnic"

Being a "Pillar" of the community...

A soft "Pillow"

Avoiding the "Pit-falls"

Taking "Pity" on those less fortunate...

Having a "Place" of your own...

Seeing His "Plan"

A full "Plate"

"Playing" with your friends...

Being a "Player" in His world...

Playful:
Full of fun and good spirits; frolicsome.
(Remember the "F", how many in this definition)

Taking a trip to the "Playground"

"Pleasant" memories...

Pleasure:
An enjoyable sensation or emotion; satisfaction; delight.

Having "Plenty"

A good "Plot"

"Plugging" the leak...

Unafraid to "Plunge" headfirst...

A "Plush" sofa...

Deep "Pockets"
(Give while there is still time)

"Poetry"

"Perhaps" the time is near'
With the Alphabet this He has made so clear,
Should we all begin to fear'
Many will not believe' What He has up His sleeve.
So prepare for yourself a "Place" just in case!

Poise:
Freedom from affection or embarrassment; dignity of manner; composure.

Polished:
To become perfect or refined; made elegant.

Being "Polite" is its own reward...

Having a "Pony"

Swimming in the "Pool"

"Popping" the question...

Being "Popular"

"Populating" the earth...

A nice "Porch"

A "Porterhouse" Steak...

A "Posh" retreat...

A "Position" of authority...

"Possessing your Possessions"

Understanding the "Possibilities"

Seeing your "Potential"

Being "Practical"

"Practice" makes "Perfect"

"Praise" Him...

"Praying" leads to many rewards...

You are "Precious" to Him...

It is all "Predestined"

His Return is "Predictable"

Choose your "Preference"

"Pregnancy" Or being "Prepared"

Enjoying His "Presence"

Being "Present" when He does return...

Giving lots of "Presents"

The ability to "Preserve" your soul...

Handling the "Pressure"

Prestige:

Prominence or influential status achieved through success; coveted status.

"Pretzels"

The ability to "Prevail"

Seeing a "Preview" of what is to come...

Knowledge of the letters is "Priceless"

Having a sense of "Pride"

"Prime Rib"

Seeing the fine "Print"

Being a "Priority"

Maintaining your "Privacy"

Feeling "Privileged"

"Privy" to the secrets...

Winning the "Prize"

Understanding the "Probability"

Solving the "Problem"

"Proceeding" with caution...

Understanding the "Process"

"Proclaiming" your loyalty...

"Procuring" your place...

The ability to "Produce" results...

Being a "Productive" member of His team...

"Professing" your beliefs...

Prolific:

Producing offspring or fruit in great abundance; fertile.

Understanding His "Promise"

He will be "Prompt"

The "Proof" is in the letters...

"Propelled" to a higher place...

Proper:
Suitable; fitting; appropriate; worthy of the name.

The ability to "Prophesy" in His name...

The ability to "Protect" what you have...

"Protecting" your loved ones...

Proud:
Of great dignity; honored; spirited.

The ability to "Provide" for your loved ones...

Getting "Published" and Chocolate "Pudding"

Having a "Pulse"

Getting a "Puppy"

Pure:
Without faults; perfect; sinless.

Having a "Purpose"

"Pursuing" your dreams...

The word "People" has two "P's";
We do serve a very significant "Purpose" in this world.
Might our sole "Purpose" be that of deciding which way we go next?

"Passing" all the test will keep you from the "Punishments"!

****

The LORD shall judge the peoples;
Judge me, O LORD, according to my righteousness,
And according to my integrity within me.
Oh, let the wickedness of the wicked come to an end,
But establish the just;
For the righteous God tests the hearts and minds.
My defense *is* of God,
Who saves the upright in heart.

PSALM 7:8-10

The letter "P" serves a profound purpose...

"Preach" the word...

Otherwise "Prepare" yourself for the "Punishments"!

PUNISHMENTS OF THE LETTER "P"

Up a Creek without a "Paddle"

Pain:
An unpleasant sensation; suffering or distress; hurting.

Turning "Pale" at His return...

Pall:
A coffin; especially one being borne to a grave or tomb.

Paltry:
Petty; trifling; insignificant; worthless.

Out of the "Pan" and into the fire...

"Pandemonium"

Panic:
A sudden, overpowering terror, often-affecting many people at once.

A "Paper" cut...

"Paralysis"

"Paralyzed" with fear...

"Paranoia"   "Parasites"   "Parched"

"Parting" ways...

Being "Passed" by...

"Passing" the buck...

"Passive"

Pathetic:
Pertaining to, expressing, or arousing pity.

Becoming the "Patsy"

Unable to see the "Pattern"

Being a "Pawn"

"Paying" your just dues...

Pelted:
To strike or assail repeatedly with or as with blows.

"Penalized"   "Penitentiary"   "Peon"

Perdition:
The loss of the soul; eternal damnation.

Peril:
A condition of imminent danger, harm or loss.

Perish:
To die, especially in a violent or untimely manner.

Are you somewhat "Perplexed" or just "Perturbed"?

"Perverse" "Pesky" and "Pestilence"

You should be "Petrified"

Stop being so "Petty"

What is your "Phobia"?

Put down the "Phone" and start "Praying"

Or are you just a "Phony"

"Phooey" on you...

Are you being "Picked" on or are you just in a "Pickle"?

He is "Picky"

"Pierced" through the Heart...

(Forget what you have been taught)

"Pillaged"

"Pimples"

In a "Pinch"

A "Pine" box...

"Pistol-whipped"

Thrown in the "Pit"

"Pitch-black"

How "Pitiful"

Plaque:
A pestilence, affliction, or calamity, originally one of divine retribution.

He will punish the whole "Planet"

Walk the "Plank"

"Plop" to your knees...

Or be "Plundered"

"Poetic" justice...

"Point-blank" range...

"Poisoned" "Poked" and thrown in the "Pokey"

"Polluted" "Pompous" and feeling "Pooped"

Is being "Poor" a Punishment?
(The meek shall inherit the earth)

Might those that have been Given Wealth
Be Being Watched to see what they do with it?

Chased by the "Posse"

A "Pound" of flesh...

Start "Pouting"

This is no "Prank"

The power of the "PRE-", the "Pretender" and
becoming "Prey" are just a few...

The outcome has been "Pre-determined"

I have seen a "Pre-view"!

"Pricked" by the sword...

Returning to a "Primitive" world...

Being a "Prisoner" in your own home...

If you are not part of the solution you are part of the "Problem"

Ease up on the "Profanity"

The "Prognosis" looks rather bleak...

"Prohibited" from entering heaven...

Incoming "Projectiles"

"Promiscuous"

"Prostitution"

"Prostrate" Cancer...

Shriveled like a "Prune"

Up in a "Puff" of smoke...

Do you feel like "Puking"?

Be with us Lord as we learn your ways...

Smashed to "Pulp"

Having no "Pulse"

"Punched" in the kidneys...

Receiving all the "Punishments"

Stop acting like a "Punk"

Time to "Punt"

Just a "Puppet"

He is in hot "Pursuit" and He is "Put-out"

"Putty" in His hands...

****

Coming to Him *as to* a living stone, rejected indeed by men,
but chosen by God *and* precious, you also, as living stones,
are being built up a spiritual house, a holy priesthood,
to offer up spiritual sacrifices acceptable
to God through Jesus Christ.
Therefore it is also contained in the Scripture,

"Behold, I lay in Zion
A chief cornerstone, elect, precious,
And he who believes on Him will by no means be put to shame."

Therefore, to you who believe,
He is precious;
but to those who are disobedient,

"The stone which the builders rejected Has
become the chief cornerstone,"

and

"A stone of stumbling
And a rock of offense."

They stumble, being disobedient to the word,
to which they also were appointed.

1 PETER 2:4-8

ALL ABOUT THE LETTER "P"

Are you a "Policeman", a "Practitioner" or a "Politician"?

"Perhaps" you have noticed the "Power" of the "P"

He has a "Prerequisite"

"Profound" enough?

"Prepare" for yourself a "Place"

"Preach" the word...

"Pretend" I can see the future...

"Possibilities" has four "I's"

"Pizza" has the double "ZZ"

The word "Expect" includes a "P" an "X" and the "T"

"Protect" yourself and your loved ones...

Try "Painting" and "Poetry"

"Pinball" "Pool" and "Protecting" your loved ones...

"Pray" often...

Father:
We Pray tonight for Guidance and Deliverance,
Let Jesus Christ be our Guide.
As we have been chosen let each one
Atone for his mistakes, But forgive for we are small.
Our faith in our LORD JESUS CHRIST will teach Us
And be our Guidance Along Your path,
For the House of Jacob will remain strong.

Amen

The "Pen" is mightier than the sword...

****

"For Moses truly said to the fathers,
"The LORD your God will raise up for you a
Prophet like me from your brethren.
Him you shall hear in all things, whatever He says to you.
'And it shall be that every soul who will not hear that Prophet
shall be utterly destroyed from among the people.'

ACTS 3:22-23

A VISIT FROM PETER PAUL AND JOHN

I wrote all day so to bed I went
Picked up the bible to search what was heaven sent
A verse or two I slowly read' when a movement
from the closet turned my head
On top of some boxes laid a purple shawl' it curled but did not fall
Was my mind playing tricks' how could this be'
this was not meant for you to see
Rolling open like a scroll' an image appeared then two'
Faces of men with beard' long robes and a side view
As they turned to show their face' another hologram appeared in place
This was John I now knew, the other two well you guess who
Four hands were raised' outstretched for thee
An image laid across the palms of those who had paid their fee
A sword I thought was being given to me'
How wrong' for it was a great pen passed from He!

"If I have told you earthly things and you do not believe,
how will you believe if I tell you heavenly things?

JOHN 3:12

QUINTESSENTIAL

RETURNING
"QUICKLY"

Q

(A thorn sticking out of the cycle of life)

A Thorn in the side...

Queasy   Quarantine   Quack

Question His power no more...

Quit stalling...

Quadruple your effort...

Quake with fear...

Qualify a place for yourself...

Quicken your approach...

Do not be: Quiet...

****

My son, do not forget my law,
But let your heart keep my commands;
For length of days and long life
And peace they will add to you.
Let not mercy and truth forsake you;
Bind them around your neck,
Write them on the tablet of your heart,
And so find favor and high esteem
In the sight of God and man.
Trust in the LORD with all your heart,
And lean not on your own understanding;
In all your ways acknowledge Him,
And He shall direct your paths.
Do not be wise in your own eyes;
Fear the LORD and depart from evil.

PROVERBS 3:1-7

A "thorn in the side" the "questions" reside
Kin to the "K" in this take pride!
"Quarantine" the litter'
Let the "Q" not make you a "Quitter"

I suppose you have a few "Questions"

240

COMMONALITY OF THE LETTER "Q"

Like it or not the letter "Q" represents something of a;
"Thorn in the Side"

Those with belief in the Lord God are however "Quintessential"!

"Quality" and "Quantity"

Fill His "Quota"

"Quarantine" the Problems...

****

Let a man so consider us,
as servants of Christ and stewards of the mysteries of God.
Moreover it is required in stewards
that one be found faithful.
But with me it is a very small thing that
I should be judged by you or by a human court.
In fact I do not even judge myself.
For I know of nothing against myself,
yet I am not justified by this;
but He who judges me is the Lord.
Therefore judge nothing before the time,
until the Lord comes,
who will both bring to light the hidden things of darkness
and reveal the counsels of the hearts.
Then each one's praise will come from God.

1 CORINTHIANS 4:1-5

"Quench" your thirst with our Lord and Savior...

"Question" those around you...

"Quarrel" no more...

The "U" follows the "Q"

**

"Quadrangle" sounds like a thorn in the side...

Learning each "Quadrant"

Having "Quadruples" sounds like it could be tough?
(Go forth and multiply, "Quantity" and "Quality")
(Teach them well, however you might want to wait)

The "Quail" can be a pain to hunt...

The "Quake" we will all soon experience...

"Qualifying" for the tournament...

"Quantum" physics...

A "Quart" a pint, a liter He does not care...
Nor does He care about the "Quarter"

Begging the "Queens" pardon...

Does this letter give us insight into the word "Queer"?

"Questions" remain...

Quest:
An act or instance of pursuing something; a search.

"Quenching" our thirst gives us difficulties...

Do you know when to add the "Question-mark"?
How difficult is it to fill out the "Questionnaire"?

How hard is it for you to remain "Quiet"?

Try knitting a "Quilt"

"Quintuples"

Solving the "Quiz" and filling the "Quota"
(Should I use "Quotations" here)?

"Quoting" a price for your soul...
"Question" His power no more...

REWARDS OF THE LETTER "Q"

Living for a "Quadrillion" years...

Having "Quadruplets"

Hunting "Quail"

Quaint:
Agreeably curious, especially in an old-fashioned way.

Surviving the "Quake"

"Qualifying" for Heaven...

Quality:
Excellence; superiority; essential character.

Producing "Quality" and "Quantity"

A "Quart" of milk...

Playing all four "Quarters"

Sacking the "Quarterback"

Owning a "Quarter-horse"

Being the "Quartermaster"

Listening to the "Quartet"

Meeting the "Queen"

Not being "Quelled"

Fulfilling His "Quest"

Having an Answer to All the "Questions"

Moving "Quickly" when the time comes...

Stepping around the "Quick-sand"

Quick-witted:
Mentally alert and sharp; keen.

Knowing when to be "Quiet"

Owning a nice "Quilt"

Quintessence:
The pure, highly concentrated essence of something.

Quintessential:
Having the nature of quintessence; pure and concentrated in nature.

"Quintuplets"

Not "Quitting" no matter how tough it gets...

Having a full "Quiver"

The ability to solve the "Quiz"

Filling His "Quota"

****

When He opened the fifth seal,
I saw under the alter the souls of those who had been slain for
the word of God and for the testimony which they held.
And they cried with a loud voice, saying,
" How long, O Lord, holy and true,
until You judge and avenge our blood on
those who dwell on the earth?"
Then a white robe was given to each of them;
and it was said to them that they should rest a little while longer,
until both *the number of* their fellow servants and their brethren,
who would be killed as they *were*,
was completed.

REVELATION 6:9-11

There is that 911 thing again...
2 CORINTHIANS 10:9-11;
(Lest I seem to terrify you by letters)

PUNISHMENTS OF THE LETTER "Q"

Quack:
An untrained person who pretends to have knowledge; a charlatan.

Becoming a "Quadriplegic"
(Remember punishments can be passed down)
(It can come from your Grandfather or your
father, mother, etc., do not judge)

Quagmire:
A difficult or precarious situation from which
extrication is almost impossible.

Caught in the "Quake"

Qualm:
A sudden feeling of sickness, faintness, or nausea.

Stuck in a "Quandary"

Being "Quarantined"

"Quarrel" no more...

Becoming the "Quarry"

Quashed:
To put down or suppress forcibly and completely.

Quaver:
To quiver, as from weakness; tremble.

Feeling "Queasy" yet?

The word "Queer" will stir up many controversies...
(Punishments handed down)?
("Query" on it)

A "Questionable" reputation...

Unable to answer the "Questions"

"Quibble" no more...

Am I moving to "Quickly"?

Stuck in the "Quick-sand"

Not knowing when to be "Quiet"

Having to be told a "Quintillion" times...

Quirk:
An unpredictable or unaccountable act or event.

Quisling:
A traitor who serves as a puppet of the enemy occupying his country.

Being a "Quitter"

"Quiver" with fear' for the time is near...

Unable to solve the "Quiz"

Not filling His "Quota"

****

**When He opened the second seal,
I heard the second living creature saying,
"Come and see."
Another horse, fiery red, went out.
And it was granted to the one who sat on
it to take peace from the earth,
and that people should kill one another;
and there was given to him a great sword.**

REVELATION 6:3-4

Because We Will not fill His "Quota"

ALL ABOUT THE LETTER "Q"

Any "Questions"?

A "Quarter" for your thoughts...

Do you believe in the "Quantum" theory?

"Quarrel" no more...

He will be here "Quickly"

Crawl under the "Quilt"

"Quench" your thirst reading the bible...

"Quit" sinning...

This is a "Quote" from above...

How often do you use the word "Quaint"?

Are you the "Quarterback", lead them well...

You must pre- "Qualify"

Be "Quick" about it...

E-Quip" yourself with the right tools...

"Question" Him no more...

****

**"These are grumblers, complainers, walking to their own lusts;
and they mouth great swelling words,
flattering people to gain advantage.
But you, beloved,
remember the words which were spoken by
the apostles of our Lord Jesus Christ:
how they told you that there would be mockers in the last time
who would walk according to their own ungodly lusts.
These are sensual persons,
who cause divisions,
not having the Spirit.
JUDE 16-19**

Notes

REMEMBRANCE

RESURRECTION

REINCARNATION

"Reality"

R

Life Exemplified; guidance required

RUDE

WRONG

Do Not "Rush" to Conclusions!

Reality belongs to the Lord God; yours might be a little bit influenced...

Reassure a place for yourself in heaven...

Respect His power...

Relinquish evil...

Return to Him...

Rest not...

Rekindle the fire...

Reincarnation is the reward...

Resurrection was the proof from our savior, Jesus Christ...

Run to Him...

Run to Him...

Run to Him...

Run to Him...

Run to Him...

****

**"I" Jesus, have sent My angel to testify to
you these things in the churches.
I am the Root and the Offspring of David,
the Bright and Morning Star."**

Revelation 22:16

*Might we sometimes have a difficult time in this world
knowing the difference between Right and Wrong because these
words both sound like they begin with the letter "R"?*

COMMONALITY OF THE LETTER "R"

Life Exemplified; Guidance Required
(A higher prospective)?

"Respect" the Word of "God"

"Re-establish" the Connection...

"Remember" the Power of the "Re"

"Rewards" begin with the letters "R" and "E"

"Receive" them all...

****

For since the creation of the world His
invisible *attributes* are clearly seen,
being understood by the things that are made,
even His eternal power and Godhead,
so that they are without excuse,
because,
although they knew God,
they did not glorify *Him* as God,
nor were thankful,
but became futile in their thoughts, and
foolish hearts were darkened.

Romans 1:20-21

*The letter "R" will give us those words that have
the tendency to give us "More"!*

The "Rabbi" has a higher calling...

The "Rabbit" and the "Raccoon" have been around for a long time...

The "Radar" shows us more...

The "Radial" tire...

The "Radiator" gives more life to the engine...

What would our world be like without the "Radio"?

The "Raft" and the "Rag" help us along...

The "Railroad" and the "Rain"

The "Raise" at work and the "Rake" for the garden...

The on and off "Ramps"

The "Ranch" and the open "Range"

The "Ranger" and the "Rank" and file...

"Rap" music...

"Rappelling" and the "Rapture"

The "Rat" and the "Ratio"

"Rations" and the "Rattlesnake"

The "Ravine" and the "Ray" of light...

"Rayon" and the "Razor"

"Reading"

The "Reams" of paper and "Reaping" what we sow...

Real:
Being or occurring in fact or actuality; having verifiable existence.

Reason/Reasoning:
A declaration made to explain or justify an action, decision, or conviction.

The "Rebate" and the "Rebel"

The "Rebirth" of our Lord and Savior...

The letter "R" is very similar to the letter "P",
Notice that they are similar in writing.
The letter "R" requires more guidance however...

The "Rear-view" mirror and the "Reactor" are prime examples.

The "Rebound" gives us another shot...

Recall:
To summon back to awareness of or concern
with the subject or situation at hand.

"Recap", "Recapture", and the "Receipt"

"Recess", "Recipe", and the "Recital"

The Power of the "RE" is "Recognizable" in the dictionary,
"Research" them with your loved ones and then "Redo" it again!

Give to the "Red Cross"

"Relay" the Message...

"Religion", "Remembering", and "Reminding" others are a few more...

The "Reservoir" and the "Resort" enhance our world...

"Respect" the power, "Restore" your faith...

A "Revelation" is life exemplified...

Rhapsody:
Exalted or excessively enthusiastic expression of feeling.

"Rhyme" and "Rhythm"

Having an extra "Rib" gave us woman...

"Rice" and being "Rich"

The "Rifle" and the "Rig"

The "Ring" on your finger...

The "River" exemplifies life for many, as do the "Roads"

The "Roller-Coaster" and the "Roman"

The "Roof" over our heads, and the "Rope"

The "Rosary" and the "Rose"

The "Roster" and the game of "Roulette"

The "Route" we choose and "Royalty"

"Rubber" and the "Ruby"

All the "Rules"

The power of the "RE" is all about a second chance;

"Redo" "Revisit" "Recall"

"Resurrection" and "Reincarnation"

"Remember" them All...

"Remember" the Power of the "P-RE"?

*You might also want to note the power of the "ER"
at the end of the words in our Language?*

****

I tell the truth in Christ,
I am not lying,
my conscience also bearing me witness in the Holy Spirit,
that I have great sorrow and continual grief in my heart.
For I could wish that I myself were accursed
from Christ for my brethren,
my countrymen according to the flesh,
who are Israelites, to whom *pertain* the
adoption, the glory, the covenants,
the giving of the law, the service *of God*, and the promises;
of whom *are* the fathers and from whom,
according to the flesh, Christ *came*,
who is over all,
the eternally blessed God.
Amen.

ROMANS 9:1-5

REWARDS OF THE LETTER "R"

Radiance:
A quality or state of being radiant; glowing; beaming.

Radiate:
To manifest in a glowing manner.

The "Radish" sounds tasty...

Might winning the "Raffle" drawing be a reward?

Raga:
A prescribed frame work of typical progressions,
Melodic formulas and rhythmic patterns...

Seeing the "Rainbow" sounds like a nice reward...

The "Raise" at work sounds rewarding?

Stand up and "Rally" for our Lord and Savior, Jesus Christ...

Might the "Rain" be a form of reward?

Owning a "Ranch" sounds nice...

Home on the "Range"

Having a high "Rank" sounds like a reward...

Rapid: Moving, acting, or occurring with great speed: swift.
Rapport: Relationship; especially, one of mutual trust or emotional affinity.

Being involved in the "Rapture" is a reward...

****

**"The Lord grant that you may find rest, each
in the house of her husband."
So she kissed them, and they lifted up their voices and wept.**

Ruth 1:9

Might He just make us a "Rare" breed?

Ratify:
To give formal sanction to; approve and so make valid.

Is getting the nice "Rating" a form of reward...

Does He just give us our daily "Rations"?

Rational: Having or exercising the ability to reason; of sound mind.

"Rationalize" this...

"Rave" about our Lord God...

The "Ravioli" sounds good, as does the "Ray of light"

The ability to "Reach" our goals sounds like a reward...

"Reacting" properly is a Reward...

"Read"

"Ready" or Not Here He Comes...

This is for "Real"

Having a true sense of "Reality" is a nice reward...

The ability to "Realize" our sins surely is a form of reward...

To "Reap" the benefits...

Reason: Good judgment; sound sense; intelligence; sanity; logical or likely.
Reasonable: Capable of reasoning; rational;
within the bounds of common sense.
Reasoning: The mental processes of one who reasons.

Might He just give us the "Reassurance" we need?

The "Rebate" sounds like a nice reward...

Be a "Rebel" with a cause...

The "Rebirth" of our Lord and Savior will be a reward for all of us...

The ability to "Rebound" sounds like a nice reward...

As does the ability to "Rebuild"

The ability to "Recall" the sacrifice of our Lord and Savior is a reward...

Let us "Recap" his life...

Will He be "Recast", of course He will...

"Receive" His rewards...
Give Him a grand "Reception"

The "Recess" at school sounds like a nice reward, as does a good "Recipe"

Being a "Recipient" of all His rewards sounds nice...

"Reciprocate" it to others...

"Reclaim" your prize...

The "Reclamation" is at hand...

The "Recliner" sure sounds comfortable...

Give Him the "Recognition" He deserves...

The ability to "Recognize" the facts is a nice reward...

Do you have any "Recollection"?

"Recommend" our Lord and Savior to others...

Give Him the "Recommendation" He deserves...

"Recommit" yourself...

"Reconcile" with the Lord God...

"Reconsider" the possibilities...

He is keeping a "Record"

"Recount" your blessings...
"Recoup" your losses...
"Recover" what was lost...
"Recreate" a life with our Lord, Jesus Christ...
"Recruit" others...
"Rectify" the problem...
"Recuperate" the losses...

How about the color "Red"

Give to the "Red Cross"

"Redeem" yourself...

"Redemption" is what it is all about...

"Redevelop" your life with Jesus Christ...

The "Re-entry" to Heaven sounds like a nice reward...

Will you be "Referred"

Refined: Free from coarseness of vulgarity; polite; gentile; precise to a fine degree.

"Reflect" on your past...

"Reform"

"Refrain" from all the temptations...

Get "Refreshed"

The "Refreshments" sound "Replenishing"

Use your "Reflexes"

Enjoy the "Refund"

With highest "Regard"

"Regardless" of what you previously heard...

"Regenerate"

With highest "Regard"

Is being "Regular" a form of reward?

Regulate: To control or direct according to a rule; to adjust to conformity.

Look up all those "Re" words in the dictionary for yourself...

(The power of the "RE")

Being able to "Resist" the temptations is surely a form of reward...

"Resistance", "Resolve", "Resounding", and "Respect", all begin with the "Re"

Taking the "Responsibility" was His sacrifice...

"Rest" while you still can...

Make a "Rendezvous" with the Lord God...

"Retrieve" for yourself the "Rest" of our "Re" words...

A "Revelation" from Jesus Christ is a powerful thing...

He "Received" all the "Rewards"

Look for His "Revival"

Rhapsody:
Exalted or excessively enthusiastic expression of feeling in speech or writing.

Might the "Rhinestone" be a reward?

Was the "Rhinosaurous" rewarded with a longer life?

How about the "Rhubarb"

Certainly having "Rhythm" is a reward...

The "Ribs" sound tasty...

How about the blue "Ribbon"

****

**"The LORD repay your work,
and a full reward be given you by the LORD God of Israel,
under whose wings you have come for refuge."**

Ruth 2-12

Is being "Rich" a form of reward, or might it be a punishment?
Might He be rewarding some believers now?
While still taking pity on those that will pay for their sins in do time?

Is being able to solve the "Riddle" a reward?

Might being able to "Ride" out the storm, be our reward?

Being "Right" is it's own reward...

The word "Righteous" speaks for itself...

Might He fill your cup to the "Rim"?

"Rise" to the occasion...

Do you own a nice "Robe"?

Robust:
Full of health and strength; vigorous; hardy; sturdy.

You are the "Rock" of His salvation...
(Especially those with the dominate "R")

Might "Rock" and "Roll" have been a reward for all of us?

The "Rod" and the Staff...

Is the ability to "Roll" with the punches a form of reward?

The "Romaine" lettuce makes for a nice salad...

"Romance" has a nice "Ring" to it...

You are so "Romantic"

Take a "Romp" through the fields...

Rosary: A string of beads on which prayers are counted...

The "Rosemary" makes for a nice spice...

Is "Receiving" the "Roses" her reward?

Is having a full "Roster" a form of reward?

Follow in the path of our Lord God and all things will turn out "Rosy"!

Being treated like "Royalty" sounds like a reward...

The "Ruby" looks brilliant...

Following all the "Rules"

"Run" to Him while you still can...

****

First, I thank my God through Jesus Christ for you all,
that your faith is spoken of throughout the whole world.
For God is my witness, whom I serve with
my spirit in the gospel of His Son,
that without ceasing I make mention of you always in my prayers,
making request if, by some means,
now at last I may find a way in the will of God to come to you.
For I long to see you, that I may impart to you some spiritual gift,
so that you may be established-
that is,
that I may be encouraged together with you by
the mutual faith both of you and me.
Now I do not want you to be unaware, brethren,
that I often planned to come to you
(but was hindered until now),
that I might have some fruit among you also,
just as among the other Gentiles.
I am a debtor both to Greeks and to barbarians,
both to wise and to unwise.
So, as much as is in me,
***I am* ready to preach the gospel to you who are in Rome also.**

Romans 1:8-15

(The Pope, two "P's" an "O" and the "E")

Use the definitions on this word...

PUNISHMENTS OF THE LETTER "R"

"Rabies"

Losing the "Race"

Being "Racial"

Strung up on a "Rack"

Listening to all the "Racket"

Is this to "Radical" for you?

Try "Radioactive"

Or set adrift in a "Raft"

Rage:
Violent anger; furious intensity, as of a storm or disease.

Ragged:
Tattered; unkempt; sloppy; imperfect.

Raided:
A surprise attack; a sudden and forcible invasion.

Not seeing the "Ramifications"

Missing the On "Ramp"

Dealing with the ensuing "Rampage"

"Rancid"

Being part of the "Rank" and file...

Held for "Ransom"

"Raped"

Getting a "Rash"

Bit by the "Rattlesnake"

"Ravaged"

263

Do you think I am just a "Raving" lunatic?

Ravenous:
Extremely hungry; voracious; greedy

Ravished:
To seize and carry away by force; raped; violated.

Razed:
To tear down or demolish; level to the ground.

Cut by the "Razor"

Slow to "React"

Unable to "Read" between the lines...

"Ready" or not here He comes...

Not knowing this is for "Real"

"Reaping" what you sow...

Dealing with the "Rebellion"

"Recaptured"

Unprepared for the "Recession"

Being a "Recipient" of all the punishments...

"Reckless" and "Reduced"

You "Reek"

Slow "Reflexes"

"Refusal" of the truth...

Being "Rejected"

"Remanded" into custody...

"Removed" from the book of life...

There are many, many more punishments that begin with the "Re",

Look them up or be "Rendered" useless...

Being "Replaced" and "Retarded" are a few more...

He will have His "Revenge"

Eating nothing but "Rice"

"Riddled" with bullets...

Stuck on the "Ridge"

"Ridiculed"

Dealing with the "Riot" and "Ripped" to shreds...

Are you willing to take the "Risk"?

Flooded by the "River"

Smothered by the "Roaches"

"Roaming" aimlessly...

"Robbed"

Struck by the "Rock"

Slammed by the "Rocket"

Smacked by the "Rod"

"Rodents"

Unable to Remember what Happened to the "Romans"

No "Roof" over your head...

Strung up by the "Rope"

"Rotting" in Hell...

"Rotten" to the core...

Sounds a little "Rough"

"Rounded" up...

265

"Routed"

Reduced to "Rubble"

Try not being so "Rude"

In a state of "Ruin"

The "Rumbling" begins...

Stop spreading "Rumors"

Unable to "Run"

Feeling "Rundown"

"Rushing" to conclusions...

"Rusting" away...

****

When He opened the third seal,
I heard the third living creature say,
"Come and see."
So I looked, and behold, a black horse,
and he who sat on it had a pair of scales in his hand.
And I heard a voice in the midst of the four living creatures saying,
A quart of wheat for a denarius, and three
quarts of barley for a denarius;
and do not harm the oil and the wine.

REVELATIONS 6:5-6

ALL ABOUT THE LETTER "R"

Might you work in the "Real Estate" Industry or for the "Rail-Road"?
You could own a "Restaurant" Or might you just like to "Read"?

The "Rock star" and the "Renegade"

"Remember" the letter "W" is part of your World also...

Sometimes you are "Right" and sometimes you are "Wrong"!

Do you work in the "Retail" Industry?

"Rest" for One day of the week...

"Research" the Alphabet...

"Rest" assured the "Rewards" are worth it!

Throw a "Roast" in the oven and teach others...

"Rekindle" the fire...

"Respect" the power...

"Rain" Or Shine He will "Return"
(Soon)

"Ready" or not...

This is for "Real"

Might you be a "Registered" Nurse or are you a "Republican?

Do not "Rush" to conclusions...

***

Rest assured the "Rewards" are worth it!
"Rowdy" and "Rude" are where the punishments will fit.
The letter "R" "Reality extreme",
Christ "Resurrected" in this we gleam...
"Life Exemplified" this is why He died!
"Reincarnation" I cried...

Notes

SOPHISTICATION

Simplicity   **Satisfaction**

S

(The "Snake" in the grass)

The Traveler in mind/body/soul...

Stubborn   **Stupid**   **Sorry**

Suppose this is truth...

Search your Soul...

Send the Message to others...

Save the Children...

Stop Sinning...

Still Skeptical...

Say it isn't So...

Salvation is your reward...

Share what you have...

****

And Hannah prayed and said:

**"My heart rejoices in the LORD;
My horn is exalted in the LORD.
I smile at my enemies,
Because I rejoice in Your salvation.
"No one is holy like the LORD,
For *there is* none besides You,
Nor *is there* any rock like our God.
"Talk no more so very proudly;
Let no arrogance come from your mouth,
For the LORD *is* the God of knowledge;
And by Him actions are weighed.**

1 Samuel 2:1-3

"Sin" Can be forgiven, unbelievers cannot...

270

COMMONALITY OF THE LETTER "S"

The "Traveler" in Mind, Body, and/or Soul...

Shall we see what the letter "S" has in "Store" for us?
Do we "Travel" to and from the "Store"?

*Will we find those that have the tendency to "travel" because their names include
The letter "S", or might it be their minds that tend to do the traveling?*

However "Subtle" it may "Seem"!

"Saddle" up or just go "Sailing"

The "Sailor" and the "Saint"

"Salmon" are always on the move...

The "Sap" oozes from the tree...

The "Saw" goes back and forth...

The Cocktail "Server" and the "Security Guard" seem to do lots of walking to and fro.

Might the "Stripper" be constantly on the move?

The "Sun" rises and "Sets" as do the "Stars" in the "Sky",

And let us not forget the tide of the "Sea"!

The "Sand" between your toes...

*The "Swimmer" and the "Shark",
The "Salesman" and your "Soul" are true "travelers"!*

How about our "Subconscious"?

Does "Sin" travel from one to another?

"Staying Strong" in the belief of Jesus Christ our "Savior" is what He wants from us!

The "Rolling stone gathers no moss"; even the "Stone" seems to travel...

**Winning "Souls" is what the "struggle"
between good and evil is all about!**

271

Is "Sex" our toughest test?

Seems that we get lots of moving around in this word also...

Might what we "Say" travel in one ear and out the other?

Travel to the nearest "Salon" or "Saloon" for that matter...

The "Snake" the "Snail" and the "Sparrow" are constantly on the move...

"Skepticism" travels throughout our minds, might it also be a punishment?

The "Starter" is what makes the car go...

The "Soldier" is constantly on the move...

The "Solicitor" moves from place to place...

Travel to the "Stadium"

The "Stallion" and the "Stamp"

The "Sailing Ship"

The "Stock-market" seems to go up and down...

The "Stop-sign" deals with the traveler...

The "Stories" we tell travel from one to another...

Does the "Storm" come and go?

The "Stream" is constantly on the move...

The "Strobe-light" goes round and round...

The "Substitute" teacher goes from place to place...

The "Subway" will take you where you need to go...

"Sweat" trickles down the face...

"Sweeping" the floor involves lots of movement...

Even the word "Stand" has something to do with the traveler...

"Saying" a prayer to the Lord God might just help us travel through eternity!

Do you do most of your traveling on "Saturday" and "Sunday"?

Your "Sense" of "Smell" travels through the air...

"Shake" rattle and roll...

"Skate" your way to Him...

"Slide" if you have to...

Do not "Slow" down...

There are no "Shortcuts" into His world…

Take the "Stairs" if you need to…

The word "So" makes your mind wander?

Does the mind travel when you "Sleep"?

There are many more "S" words "still" left for you...

Travel to your nearest Dictionary and "Settle" by the fire...

"Save Your Soul"

The Lord God "Saves" us in two very unique ways...

Either our "Souls" are saved and are "Sent" to heaven...

Or

He saves our Lives here on earth for the long haul...

"See" You At the House of Jacob...

****

**"Now, O LORD GOD,
the word which You have spoken concerning Your servant
and concerning his house,
establish *it* forever and do as You have said.**

2 Samuel 7:25

REWARDS OF THE LETTER "S"

The "Sabbath" day or might it just be the "Sabbatical"?

Feeling "Safe" and the ability to "Safeguard" your loved ones...

"Safety" first...

The "Sage" on the beef sounds like a reward...

Being referred to as a "Saint" sounds rewarding...

Is "Saint Patrick's Day" a reward for the Irish?

Would you care for a "Salad" with that?

Might the "Salary" you get from work be a form of reward?
Or does it just tend to do lots of traveling?

Enjoy the "Sale"!

"Salutations"

The ability to "Salvage" what was lost sounds like a reward...

"Salvation" speaks for itself...

Be a good "Samaritan"!

The ability to "Sample" before you buy...

"Sanctify" Him...

Might the "Sand-lot" be a reward for the children?

Time for a "Sandwich"

Keeping your "Sanity"

"Santa Claus"

(Enjoy this life He has given to us)

The "Sapphire" you are wearing?
(How much is enough)?

The "Satin Sheets"

The ability to "Satisfy"

The Barbecue "Sauce" and "Sautéed" food of any kind.

I'll have the "Sausage"

Enjoy the "Sauna"

Becoming "Saved"!

How Much do you Need in your "Savings" account?

****

**"Do not lay up for yourselves treasures on earth,
where moth and rust destroy and where thieves break in and steal:
"but lay up for yourselves treasures in heaven, where neither moth
nor rust destroys and where thieves do not break in and steal.
"For where your treasure is, there your heart will be also.**

Matthew 6:19-21

*

Become a "Savior"!

"Savor" the taste...

Might He just reward us with the "Savvy" to understand?

The ability to "Say" what you feel...

The ability to "Scale" new heights...

The "Scenery" is a beautiful reward as is the "Scent" of a woman...

"Scholarly"

One "Scoop" or two...

He "Scores"

Have a "Scotch and Soda"

Understanding the "Scripture"

"Scrutinize" the Alphabet!

"Search" for the truth...

The ability to "Sculpture"

"Security"

"Seek" and you shall find...

"Seize" the moment...

The "Select" few...

*There are many rewards and punishments that begin with the word "Self",
Look them up in the dictionary!*

"Send" the Message to others...

I feel "Sensational"!

Does it all make "Sense"?

Be "Sensible"!

How "Sensuous"

Follow the "Sequence" of events...

"Serenade" her...

How "Serene"

He is "Serious"

Become His "Servant"

The next "Session" has started...

He will "Settle" it once and for all...

"Sexuality", "X" marks the spot...

Might finding the "Shade" be a form of reward,
it is constantly on the move however.

"Shameless"

The ability to "Share"

Finding the "Shelter"

We are no longer "Shielded" by innocence...

"Shine" for all to see...

"Show" Him you believe!

A nice hot "Shower" might be considered a reward?
(The water travels down)

How "Shrewd" is He?

"Shrimp" cocktail anyone...

Was your "Sibling" a reward or punishment?

"Stand by His "Side"
"Set your "Sights" on Him...
"Signify" His return...

Do not be "Silent"

Where do you hide the fine "Silver"?

He can make life much "Simpler"

Be "Sincere"!

"Sing" with all your heart...

Having a "Sister" is a nice reward...

The ability to "Sketch" and the ability to "Ski"
(Do you recognize the "traveler" in these two words)?

"Skim" milk...

Might the color of your "Skin" be a reward?

"Skinny-dipping" might be another...

Nice "Skirt"

The blue "Skies" are a reward for us all...

A clean "Slate"

Sleek:
Smooth and lustrous as if polished; tailored in appearance.

"Sleep" well...

A "Slice" of pie...

A good "Slogan"

He is "Smart"

A beautiful "Smile" goes a long way...

A "Smooth" ride...

Enjoy the "Smorgasbord"

Are you nice and "Snug"?

"Soar" with the eagles...

Try staying "Sober" occasionally...

"Socialize"

A warm pair of "Socks"

The word "Soft" has a nice ring to it...

Fertile "Soil"

Take "Solace" in Him...

Solemn:
Deeply earnest; serious: Of impressive nature.

Solid:
Sound; reliable; concrete: Upstanding and dependable.

"Solidify" your Place in Heaven!

Is "Solitude" a Reward or Punishment?
Might it be a form of reward at times, while
still being a punishment for others?

Going" "Solo" has its Rewards...

The Summer "Solstice"

He does have a "Solution"

"Solve" the mystery...

Be one of the "Some"!

"Some-day" soon...
"Some-one" you know...
"Some-where"

"Sooner" than you think!

Might having a "Son" be a Great Reward?
(The Daughter Too)

"Sophisticated" is a long word...

"Soup or Salad"?
Extra "Sour Cream"
"Sourdough Bread"

Reap what you "Sow"

Find "Space" in this world for Him!

Heaven is "Spacious" enough for even you...

Don't forget the "Spaghetti"
What might the "double tt" in this word mean?
Might it be that we just tend to eat lots of it?

"Span" the universe...

Help "Spare" someone you know!

The "Sparkle" in her eyes...

"Speak" the word...

You are "Special"

He does have a "Specific" agenda...

It will be "Spectacular"

Does He need to "S P E l l " it out?

"Spend" wisely, give...

"Spew" forth...

Add some "Spice"

High "Spirits"

"Spirituality" and "Splashing" in the pool...
(Can you see the traveler)?

Splendor:
Great light or luster; brilliance: Glorious; Illustrious.

"Sponsor" the Homeless...

Give more than a "Spoonful"

"Spontaneity"

Be a good "Sport"

"Sportsmanship"

"Stand in the Spotlight"

"Spotless"

Might having a loving "Spouse" be a form of reward?

"Spread" the word, let it "travel"

"Sprinkle" it with love...

Stability:
Constancy of character or purpose; steadfast.

"Stake" your place in heaven...

"Speaking of Steak"

Steady:
Reliable; Dependable: Stable; Fixed.

"Steep" is the price...

"Step" up to the plate...

The "Step-Sister"

A pot of "Stew"

"Stick" to your beliefs...

Do you have the "Stomach" for it?

Tell His "Story"!

Stout:
Determined, bold, or brave; sturdy.

"Straight" is His path...

He does have a "Strategy"

"Strawberries and Sugar" sounds like a tasty reward...

"Streamline" your efforts...

Find the "Strength"

A "Strike" in bowling...

"Strive" for perfection...

Be "Strong"

"Structure"

Be a "Stud" in His world...

"Study" the bible...

Sturdy:
Substantially built; durable; strong, robust.

A sense of "Style"

Suave:
Smoothly gracious in social manner; urbane.

"Subdue" those around you with the Power of the Alphabet!

Sublime:
Characterized by nobility; grand; majestic.

The ability to "Succeed" is a form of reward...

"Succulent" and "Sufficient" are two more...

Enjoy the "Summer"

Make "Sunday" your "Sabbath" or any other day you choose...

Super:
Of great value or excellence; extraordinary.

He is "Superior"!

The last "Supper"

"Support" one another...

Reign "Supreme"!

Becoming "Sure" of yourself...

The ability to "Surge" ahead...

The ability to "Surpass" others...

"Surprise" those around you, "Surrender" to Him...

Enjoying your "Surroundings"

The ability to "Survive"

The ability to "Sway" others...

How "Sweet" it is...

Having "Sympathy" for others less fortunate...

Maple "Syrup" please...

"Satisfy" His Requirements and Receive All the Rewards!

****

**Then Samuel spoke to all the house of Israel,
saying,
"If you return to the LORD with all your hearts,
then
put away the foreign gods and the
Ashtoreths from among you,
and prepare your hearts for the LORD,
and serve Him only;
and He will deliver you from the hand of the Philistines."**

1 Samuel 7:3

***

**So David said to all his servants who
were with him at Jerusalem,
"Arise, and let us flee,
or we shall not escape from Absalom.
Make haste to depart,
lest he overtake us suddenly and bring disaster upon us,
and strike the city with the edge of the sword".**

2 Samuel 15:14

WILLIAM E. BEAVERS

**

A squadron of planes flying low from the past
This vision from Pearl Harbor' in my mind it does last.
The souls of those pilots felt'
Though then the clouds did start to melt!

****

My son, keep my words,
And treasure my commands within you.
Keep my commands and live,
And my law as the apple of your eye.
Bind them on your fingers;
Write them on the tablet of your heart.
Say to *wisdom*, "You *are* my sister,"
And call understanding *your* nearest kin,
That they may keep you from the immoral woman,
From the seductress *who* flatters with her words.

PROVERBS 7:1-5

PUNISHMENTS OF THE LETTER "S"

Sabotage:
Any underhanded effort to defeat or do harm to an endeavor.
(Do not let those that disbelieve "sabotage" His sacrifice)!

Sacrilege:
The misuse, theft, desecration, or profanation of anything
consecrated to a deity or regarded as sacred.

Are you feeling a little "Sad"?

"Sadism" and "Sadistic"

Do not "Sag" behind...

Do not be a "Sap"

Lighten up on the "Sarcasm"

"Satan"!

Are you feeling a little "Saturated" about now?

The Indians were "Savage"

"Scabies", "Scalded", and "Scalped" are forms of punishment...

Being involved in the "Scandal"

Scant:
Deficient in quantity or amount; meager; inadequate.

Do not be the "Scapegoat"

I have many "Scars"

Might He just make us "Scarce"?

Are you "Scared" yet?

Might He just "Scatter" us...

You will be "Scoffed" at!

Have you "Scolded" your Child lately?

"Scorched"

Why is He so "Scorned"
(Might this be Evil at work)?

Scourge:
Any means of inflicting severe suffering, vengeance, or punishment.

He is "Scowling" at us...

Do you look a little "Scraggly"?

Do not let the "Scratch" become infected...

The "Scud" missile can inflict lots of punishment...

Stop all the "Scuffling"

The "Scum" of the Earth...

"Scurvy"

Seared:
To make withered; dried up or shriveled: To char; scorched.

Might you just be "Secluded" from those that believe?

You may not get a "Second" Chance, Accept Him Now!
Do not be "Seduced" by unrighteousness...
See what you Have been missing!
Seek and you shall find.

The "Seizure" comes suddenly...

"Self-absorbed", Self-denial", and "Selfish"
Are just a few of the punishments for those that think only of themselves!

Do not "Sell" yourself short...

Is "Senility" a form of punishment for those that have attained an older age?

Are you feeling a little "Sensitive"?

Is the criminal punished with a harsh "Sentence"?

"Separation" from truth...

"Settling" for less than you deserve...

His punishments can be "Severe"!

Indiscriminate "Sex" causes many...

"Shabby", Shackled", and getting the "Shaft" are a few...

"Shake" with fear, for the time is near!

How "Shallow" are you?

"Shame" on you...

"Shape-up" or "Ship-out"

Have I "Shattered" your illusions?

Where did you get that "Shiner"?

Do not "Shirk" your responsibilities...

Do you feel like "Shit" about now?

"Shiver" with fear, for the time is near!

Are you in "Shock"?

Life is "Short"!

Have you ever been "Shot"?

Quit "Shoving"

Do not be such a "Show-off"

Torn to "Shreds"

"Shudder" with fear for the time is near!

"Shunning" your responsibilities...

Are you feeling "Sick"?

When was the last time your car was "Side-swiped"?

This country is already under "Siege"!

How can you remain "Silent"!
(That is just plain "silly")

"Sinking" to a new level...

"Sinus" problems...

"Six-Six-Six"!

The "Size" of your belief is all that matters...

You must not be a "Skeptic"

"Skidding" out of control...

Are you a little "Skittish"?

Are you a "Slacker"?

When was the last time you had the door "Slammed" in your face?

Stop with all the "Slander"

A "Slap" in the face...

A "Slashed" throat...

Might He just "Slaughter" us all?

Is "Slavery" a form of Punishment?

"Slay" your disbelief...

Try not to be so "Sleazy"

Are you a "Slime-ball"?

Try not to "Slip" and fall...

Slop:
Unappetizing, watery food or soup; waste.

Is your homework "Sloppy"?

Do not be such a "Slouch"

Are you a "Slow-poke"?

I feel a little "Sluggish" today...

Smart aleck:
One who is obnoxiously self-assertive and arrogant.

"Smashed" to pieces...

You "Smell"

He can "Smite" us anytime He so chooses...

Might the "Smog" be a form of punishment for our ways?

"Smothered" to death...

Snafu:
In a state of complete confusion; chaotic.

"Snatched" right from under your nose...

Sneak:
To behave in a cowardly or servile manner; underhanded.

What a "Snob"

Snub:
To treat with scorn or contempt; slight by
ignoring or behaving coldly toward.

"Solitary" confinement...

Are you a little "Sore"?

Say your "Sorry", and Save your Soul!

Did you deserve the "Spanking"?

"Spill" the beans, tell others...

Spiteful:
Filled with or prompted by spite; malicious.

"Spoiled", "Spurned", "Squabble", "Squashed",
"Stagger", "Stained", "Stale", and the "Stalker" are a few more.

Watch out for the "Stampede"

*Why are there those in this country that are "Starving"?
(Might you be Next)?*

Thou Shall Not "Steal"!

The price is "Steep"

The "Stench" of the dead...

Have you gotten yourself in a "Sticky" situation?

It "Stings" doesn't it!

You Can be forgiven; all it takes is a "Sincere" Commitment!

How can you be so "Stingy"?

You "Stink"

Throw them in the "Stockade"

The "Storm" is a warning...

As is getting "Stranded"

The word "Stress" has the double "SS"

Might you need a "Stretcher"?

Have you been "Stricken" with the flu?

He will "Strike" again "Soon"

Might the "Stroke" be a form of punishment?

*All our "Struggles" are punishments!
(The double "GG" in this word)*

"Stumble" and fall...

*Stupidity:
Showing a lack of sense or intelligence.*

Do not be "Stupid"; Accept Him as your Lord and Savior!

Sucker:
One who is easily deceived; a gullible person; dupe.

He will come "Suddenly", will you be prepared?

Otherwise "Suffer" the consequences...

There is no need to "Sulk" if you believe...

Sullen:
Showing a brooding ill humor or resentment; morose; sulky.

Are you a little "Superficial"?

Do Not let Him be "Suppressed"!

Surly:
Sullenly rude and ill humored; brazenly uncivil; gruff.

"Surrender" to Him...

The "Swarm" of locust...

The "Swelling" in your feet...

Have you ever been "Swindled"

"Switch" sides...

Cut by the "Sword"

He has no "Sympathy" for unbelievers...

Are you feeling the "Symptoms"?

Might "Syphilis" be a punishment for indiscretion?

**

There are many, many more punishments beginning with the letter "S"
Might this be due to the fact the word "Sex" starts with this letter?
Or is it just the fact that the "letter "S" does lots of traveling?

Follow the Ten...

Refraining from unrighteousness is where it "Starts"!

Just do the best you can and do not worry about being
judged by anyone other than our **Lord Jesus Christ.**

****

So David went on and became great,
and the Lord God of Hosts was with him.

2 SAMUEL 5:10

ALL ABOUT THE LETTER "S"

The "Salesman", "Security Guard" and the
"Scientist" begin with the letter "S"

"Stop Sinning & Save the Soul"

"So" Much for Tomorrow...

"Silent" prayers are nice...

"Spend" some time with those you love...

"Serve" up some "Spaghetti" and a "Soda"

"Spirituality" is a wonderful thing...

"See" for yourself...

**"Search" the Dictionary what will you find'
the "Traveler" in "Soul", Body, or Mind...
The letter "S" this definition "Set", The "Star" of David I have met.
Finding Christ is His desire, "Swim" not in the lake of fire!**

"Sing" to/for Him...

"Snuggle" up with a good book...
(He "sees" when we read the bible)
(Remember the two B's)?

Do not "Say" that He did not warn us...

"Spread" the word...

"Start" saving what you will need...

"Shoes" and "Socks" might come in handy?

Hope you like "Sushi"

Are you "Spinning" out of control?

"Sing" Loud

Notes

TRIUMPHANT

Truth

Trust

The Test

T t

Tribulation, tough times, tests...

Temptation

Tribulation

Tragedy

****

and they will turn *their* ears away from the
truth, and be turned aside to fables.

2 TIMOTHY 4:4

The Year Two Thousand Ten Has Three Capitol T's!

Try Turning over a new leaf...

Test after Test...

Test after Test...

Test after Test...

Test after Test...

Test after Test...

How many times has mankind failed in the past?

When will we learn?

Now the glory of God of Israel had gone up from the cherub,
where it had been,
to the threshold of the temple.
And He called to the man clothed with linen,
who *had* the writer's inkhorn at his side;
and the LORD said to him,
"Go through the midst of the city,
through the midst of Jerusalem,
and put a mark on the foreheads of the men who sigh and
cry over all the abominations that are done within it."

EZEKIEL 9:3-4

The letter "T" is one of those letters in our vocabulary
which gives us "two" very Unique clues...

The capitol "T" tends to give us many good, as well as tough words in our world;
(Tough love from our Lord God)

Might the Lord God have control over the capitol "T"?
(The Lord rules above, no sign of Man or Evil)

Might the lower case "t" tend to represent the sacrifice of His son?
Our Savior Jesus Christ?

Only He has all the answers...

Is it possible that those words in our language with the double "tt" give us our,
"Toughest times"

As we dive into the letter "T" we will examine this unusual phenomenon first.

"Attack", "Battle", "Bitter", "Butter", "Little" and "Lottery" speak for themselves;
How about the words "Cattle", "Cigarette", "Better" and "Tattoo",
Do we understand the "tribulation" in each of these words?

How many cattle are slaughtered each year to feed mankind?
How many of us die, or fall ill do to smoking?

How "tough" is it to try to do "Better", and as for the word
"Tattoo", does this fit into The Bible teachings of "Thou shall
not desecrate thy body", or is it just simply painful?

The "Attorney", "Litter", "Ghetto" and the "Gutter" are a few more...

The word "Letters"
The City of "Seattle"
The City of "Pittsburgh"

"Gettysburg"

The "Lettuce" will wilt rather quickly...

Take the time to see how many other double letter "tt" words you can find...

P.S. Do not forget to replace the "Batteries"!

297

WILLIAM E. BEAVERS

Notes

COMMONALITY OF THE LETTER "T"

The "T" Represents "Tribulation", through and through...

*How many words in our English Dictionary that starts with
the letter "T" will give us The Tendency for "Tribulation"*

Twin Towers   Titanic   Teeth   Traffic   Taxes

Tough   Tornado   Tsunami   Terrible Tragedy   Temptation

These are just a few of our words that represent the letter "T"!

*"Teach" our children well, "take the time" to
instill upon them the sacrifice of;*

"Jesus Christ"

**

Our Toughest Times...

How soon are the "Tabs" due on your vehicle?

"Tabasco" can be tough on the palate...

The word "Taboo" speaks for itself...

Ask the running back, he will tell you the "Tackle" is tough on the body.

Does the "Tadpole" have a tough time?

How tough is it to eat the "Taffy"?

How tough is it to get to the child when we play "Tag"?

When was the last time you were "Tailgated"?

"Take-home pay", might it be a little tougher after all the deductions?

Listening to the one who "Talks" to much, can be tough on the ears...

Does being to "Tall" have its tough times?

The "Talon" of a bird of prey sounds like it can be tough...

The "Tank" sounds like it gives us lots of tough times...

*The Dinosaur will tell you the "Tar" was tough,
or is it just tough to "Tar" the roof?*

Being a "Target" sounds like it is full of tribulation...

How about the "Tarot" cards?

The word "Tax" says it all; "X" marks the spot...

How tough is it to form a good "Team"?

The "Tears" we cry at night are due to tough times...

Might things just be to "Technical" for us?

How much "tribulation" is there in the word "Technology"?

*The "Teenagers" life is full of tough times!
Help Guide them...*

*How much "Tribulation" do we have with the
"Telephone" and the "Television"?
(The Commandments teach us, thou shall not
have any other idols before God,
Do we have a tendency to put these two things before our Lord)!*

"Temptation" will lead us to sin...

The "Ten Commandments" are definitely "tough" to follow!

The "Term" paper takes all night to finish...

The "Terrain" can be rocky...

*Terrible: Causing terror or fear; dreadful:
To fill with terror; make deeply afraid; to alarm.*

*Terror: Intense, overpowering fear.
Terrorism, speaks for itself...*

The "Test" begins and ends with the letter "T"!

When was the last time you had to "Testify" in court?

Or write out a sworn "Testimony"?

"Texas" begins with the capitol "T"
("X" marks the spot)...

"Theft" is a sin...

Might (I/You) need to visit the "Therapist"?
(How many times do they listen to tough times)?

"Thirst" and the "Thorn" both begin with the letter "T"!

Have you ever been "Threatened"?

How often do you get a sore "Throat"?

How tough is it getting "Through" the letter "T"?

"Throw away" your previous beliefs...

Might we need to be a little more careful on "Tuesday" and "Thursday"?

How much did your last "Ticket" cost you?

Watch out the "Tide" is coming in...

Are your pants to "Tight", or are you just on "Tilt"?

"Timber"

"Time" is one of the "toughest" words we face...

"Tiny"

Are you getting "Tired" yet?

Might your "Tire" be flat?

The "Titanic" and the "Twin Towers" put a lot
of people through "tough" times!

TNT...(Ka-Boom)!

Have you ever kissed a "Toad"?

Have you ever burned the "Toast"?

301

Have you ever stubbed your "Toe"?

Let us not forget the "Toddler"

"Tobacco"

The "Toilet" just about covers it...

Do not forget to pay the "Toll"

How about the "Tomahawk"

Watch your "Tongue"

How tough is it to find the right "Tool"?

When was the last time you went to the Dentist to have a "Tooth" pulled?

"Torah" begins with the "T"

*"Torment", "Tornado", "Torpedo", "Torrential", "Tortoise", and "Torture"
(The letter "T" is "Tough")!*

How tough is it to score the winning "Touchdown"?

"Tournament" and the "Tourniquet"

"Tracheotomy" speaks for itself...

How tough is it to get around the race "Track"?

*The word "Trade" has many definitions...
The World "Trade" Center...*

*Traditor:
One of the early Christians who betrayed fellow Christians
during the Roman persecutions.*

****

**Therefore do not be ashamed of the testimony of our Lord,
nor me in the sufferings for the gospel
according to the power of God.**

2 TIMOTHY 1:8

The word "Traffic" also has the double "ff"

Try not to get lost on the "Trail"

The "Trailer" and the "Train" start with the letter "T"

How tough is it to complete the "Transaction"?

How tough is it to "Transcribe" the letter you are working on?

Reading the "Transcript" can be tough...

How tough was it the last time you had to "Transfer" to another plane?

Making the "Transformation" to a life with Jesus Christ can be "tough"!

The "Transfusion" sounds tough too...

Transgression:
The violation of a law, command, or duty.

How tough is the life of the "Transient"?
(Another of our words that begins and ends with the "T")!

How tough will it be for you to make the "Transition"?

The "Translation" was tough to comprehend...

The "Transplant" sounds tough...

Watch out for the "Trap"

Do not forget to take out the "Trash"
(Sounds like a punishment)

"Traveling" to "Heaven" might be a little tough...

Do not "Tread" on Me...

Can we be punished for the "Treatment" we give others, of course we can?

"Treason" sounds tough, as does the "Treaty"!

How about all the tough times with the "Tree"
When was the last time someone you knew fell out of the "Tree house"?
How many "Trees" does it take to make all the paper we use?

The "Tree" of life...

Can the Power of our Lord God make you "Tremble"?

The "Tremor" is just a warning...

Down in the "Trenches"

No "Trespassing"

How long will this "Trend" last?

Being part of the "Triad" sounds pretty tough...

Ask a few people about the "Trials" they have been through...

The Lord God understands about "Trial and Error"!
(The Double "RR" in error)

The "Tribe" of Indians certainly went through some tough times...

"Tribulation" sounds like a word from God!

Let us not forget to pay "Tribute" to our Lord...

A "Trick" or a "Treat"?
(A punishment or a reward)?

The "Trigger" gives us lots of tough times...

Do you need to be told for the "Trillionth" time?

The "Third" "Trimester"

Do not "Trip" and fall...

A "Trip" to the Dentist...

"Triplets"

The "Triton" submarines...

The "Troglodyte" is an interesting word, how about the "Troll"
(Did He make them extinct)?

Do our "Troops" in Iraq face tough times ahead?

Trouble:
A state of distress, affliction, danger, or need.

Pull up your "Trousers"

How tough is it for the "Truck" driver...

What is in the "Trunk"?

"Try" to do better that is what our Lord God is after!

The "Tryout" seems like it's a little tough...

We have all seen how tough the "Tsunami" can be...

"Tuberculosis" causes many tough times...

When was the last time you took a "Tumble"?

The "Tummy" and the "Tumor" are "T" words...

You try to carry the "Tune"

When was the last time your car had a "Tune up"?

Let us hope the "Tunnel" does not collapse...

The "Turf" is what the gangster is fighting for...

"Turkey" for dinner, anyone?

Do not forget to "Turn off" the stove...

He is such a "Turn off"

How was the "Turn out" for your last reception?

You need to pay the "Toll" when taking the "Turnpike"

Taste like "Turpentine"

The "Turret" and the "Turtle" both begin with the letter "T"

The "Twelve" Apostles have definitely had their share of tough times...

Getting "Twenty-one" in the game of Blackjack can be tough...

How tough is it to be a "Twin"?

Do not be such a "Twit"

Might it be tough for you to do the "Typing"?

Typhoon   Tyrannosaurus   Tyrant

**Therefore, brethren,
stand fast and hold the traditions which you were taught,
whether by word or our epistle.**

2 THESSALONIANS 2:15

REWARDS OF THE LETTER "T"

Tabernacle:
The portable sanctuary in which the Jews carried the
Ark of the Covenant through the desert.

Might the "Table" we eat from be our reward or is it the "Tablecloth"?

Tack:
A course of action meant to minimize opposition to the attainment of a goal.

Tact:
The ability to appreciate the delicacy of a situation
And to do or say the kindest or most fitting thing.

The word "Take" has many definitions...

Talent:
A mental or physical attitude; specific natural or acquired ability.

Tame:
Naturally gentle or unafraid.

How about the ability to get a nice "Tan"

Tangible:
Capable of being exactly comprehended.

Taste:
To experience or partake of, especially for the first time; to like.
Tasty: Having a pleasing flavor; savory.

The "T-bone" sounds very tasty so does the "Iced Tea"

The ability to "Teach" sounds like a nice reward...

Technique:
The degree of skill or command of fundamentals.

Is "Technology" a form of reward?

How about the "Teddy Bear"

*The Ability to "Tell" Everyone About Our Savior
Jesus Christ is Definitely a Reward!*

****

**Therefore he who rejects this does not reject man,
but God,
who has also given us His Holy Spirit.**

1 THESSALONIANS 4:8

*Temperament:
The manner of thinking, or behaving characteristic of an individual.
Temperance: Moderation or self-restraint.*

Might the "Temple" be our reward?

*Tenable:
Capable of being defended or sustained; logical.*

Might being "Tenacious" be a form of reward...

*Tender/Tenderness:
Having a delicate quality; expressing gentle emotions.*

*Tenderhearted:
Easily moved by another's distress; compassionate.*

The "Tenderloins" sound juicy...

Can He reward us "Tenfold"?

Is the ability to play "Tennis" a form of reward?

How about the "Tent"?

*Tenure:
The holding of something such as real state or office; occupation.*

The "Teriyaki" sounds inviting...

*Terrific:
Very good or fine; splendid; magnificent.*

Being able to pass the "Test" sounds like a reward from the LORD...

Reading the New "Testament" might lead us to many rewards...

"Testifying" about Jesus Christ leads us to Eternity...

Testimonial/Testimony:
A formal or written statement "Testifying" to truth or fact!

Might giving "Thanks" to our Lord God give us our Rewards!

"Thanksgiving Day" sounds like a nice feast.

"Thawing" out the Ice Age might have been a nice reward for humankind?

"Theology"
The study of the nature of God and Religious Truth;
Rational inquiry into Religious questions,
especially those posed by Christianity.

Therapy:
The treatment of illness or disability in physical therapy or psychotherapy.

Thereafter:
From a specified time onward.

Might our Reward be that of a good "Thesis"?

That ability to "Think" is definitely a Reward...

Thorough: *Fully done; finished; completely as described: absolute.*
Thoroughbred: *Thoroughly trained or educated; well bred.*
Thoughtful: *Showing regard for others; considerate.*
Threefold: *Three times as much or as great.*
Thrifty: *Wisely economical; frugal.*

Thrill:
To cause to feel a sudden intense sensation; excite greatly.

How about going to the "Three-Ring" circus...

Is the "Thumb" a Reward for humankind?

Tickle:
To touch lightly with a tingling sensation causing laughter.

Tidings:
Information; news.

Tidy:
Orderly and neat in appearance or procedure

Is having the "Time" its own Reward?

Timeless:
Independent of time; unending; eternal; ageless.
(Sounds like our Lord God here)

Is having good "Timing" a form of reward?

Is having that good "Tingling" feeling a form of reward?

Is getting the good "Tip" a reward?

Tiptop:
The highest degree of quality or excellence.

Might working "Tirelessly" be a form of reward?

Is having the "Title" to your vehicle a reward?

Is living for "Today" His reward to us?

The "Toffee" sounds sweet...

Tolerable/Tolerance/Tolerant/Tolerate:
The capacity for or practice of allowing or respecting the nature,
beliefs, or behavior of others.

The "Tomato" sounds juicy...

Having the right "Tool" for the job might be a form of His rewards...

Use the Alphabet as a "Tool" to learn and teach...

Being at the "Top" sounds nice...

The "Tortilla" sounds good...

Total:
Complete; utter; absolutely; entirety.

Having a nice "Touch" sounds like a nice reward...

Might having all the good "Toys" be a reward?

The ability to "Trace" your path sounds like a nice reward...

"Trade" places with our savior "Jesus Christ"!

Tradition:
A mold of thought or behavior followed by a people continuously
from generation to generation.

Tranquil/Tranquility:
Free from agitation or other disturbance; calm; unruffled; serene.

The ability to "Translate" sounds like a nice reward...

The ability to "Travel" sounds like a nice reward...

Finding the "Treasure" is surely a reward...

The word "Treat" has many definitions...

Will paying "Tribute" to our Lord God get us His Rewards?

Trinity:
The Union of Three Divine Figures, the Father, Son, and the Holy Ghost.

Might being able to make the "Trip" be our reward?

Might the "Triple Play" be a reward?

Triumph/Triumphant
Exulting in success or victory; conquering; magnificent; splendid.

The word "Trophy" speaks for itself...

The word "Tropical" sounds nice...

The "Trout" sounds tasty...

True/Truth:
Consistent with fact or reality; not false or erroneous; honorable; upright.

Trust:
Firm reliance on the integrity, ability or character of a person or thing; faith.

What He asks from us is that we "Try"

Might it be your "Turn" to receive the Rewards?

"Turnover" a new leaf...

"Turquoise" has a nice color...

"Tutti-frutti" is a nice flavor...

"Twilight" sounds pleasing...

The "Twinkle" in her eyes...

****

She bore a male Child who was to rule all nations with a rod of iron.
And her Child was caught up to God and His throne.

REVELATION 12:5

And the dragon was enraged with the woman,
and he went to make war with the rest of her offspring,
who keep the commandments of God and
have the testimony of Jesus Christ.

REVELATION 12:17

The letter "T" is "Tough" you'll see' a "Test" for thee?
"Tribulation" through and through!
The "Twin Towers" and the "Titanic" too...
The "Tornado" and the "Tsunami" are more of these
Punishments for our sins, the "Truth" in this' He sees...
Pass them all' "Triumphant" is where it leads.
Be "Tempted" not' do many good deeds!

PUNISHMENTS OF THE LETTER "T"

Taboo: A prohibition excluding something from use,
Approach, or mention because of its sacred and inviolable nature.

Tacky: Marked by neglect and disrepair; run-down; shabby.
Tactless: Lacking in delicacy; bluntly inconsiderate.
Taint: To stain the honor of someone or something.

Can He "Take" away our Rewards; of course He can...

Tale: A malicious story, piece of gossip.
Talkative: Having an inclination to talk too much.
Tamper: To interfere in a harmful manner; to meddle foolishly.
Tangle: To involve in hampering or awkward complications; entangle.

Tantalize:
To tease or torment by or as if by exposing to view,
But keeping out of reach something much desired.

Tardy: Occurring, arriving, or acting latter than expected or scheduled; late.
Tarnish: To dull the luster of; to spoil or taint.
Tart: Having a sharp pungent tasty; sour.

The "Task" at hand seems awful punishing...

Tasteless: Lacking flavor; poor taste; insipid.
Tatter: Torn and ragged; a shred.
Tattle: To chatter aimlessly; to reveal through gossip.
Taunt: To deride or reproach with content; mock; jeer at.
Tawdry: Gaudy and cheap; vulgarly ornamental.
Tear: To pull apart or into pieces; to rip; to divide or disunite.
Tease: To annoy; pester; vex; to arouse hope, desire, or curiosity without satisfaction.
Tedious: Tiresome or uninteresting by reason of extreme slowness; monotonous.
Temper: A tendency to become easily angry or irritable.

Do not be "Tempted" by evil!

Tense/Tension: Nerve-racking; suspenseful; tightly strained.

Does He have the Ability to "Terminate" us as a form of His Punishments?

Can we pass the "Test"?

Are you getting a little "Testy"?

Do not be "Thick" headed...

Thief: A person who steals property or commits larceny.
Thin-skinned: Oversensitive, especially to reproach or insult.
Thirsty: Desiring to drink; arid; parched.

Thirty Years' War
A series of religious wars fought in Europe.

Thorn: A person or thing that causes sharp pain, irritation, or discomfort.
Thoughtless: Careless; unthinking; reckless; rash; inattentive; inconsiderate.

Can He "Threaten" us with our very existence?

Can He punish us "Three-fold"?

Does He punish us "Through" and "Through"?

Might He just "Throw" us away?

Might He just give us the "Thug"?

The "Thumb-screw" sounds punishing...

Maybe He'll just give us a "Thumping"?

Might the "Thunder" be a warning?

"Tick", "Tock", the clock is "Ticking"

Might the "Ticket" you just got for speeding be a punishment?

The "Tidal Wave" sounds awful punishing...

The "Tiger" can cause lots of punishment...

Do not be a "Tight-wad", give when you can...

Are you on "Tilt"?

Not having enough "Time" to do the things we want Is a form of

His punishment...

"Time" is of the Essence...

Tipsy: Likely to tip over; unsteady; crooked.
Tirade: A long violent or blustering speech, especially when censorious or denouncing.
Tired: Worn-out; fatigued; overused.
Toil: To proceed or make ones way with difficulty, pain, or exhaustion.

Might "Today" Be the day He punishes us?

Might He punish us "Tomorrow"?

Might He punish us "Tonight"?

Hit by a "Ton" of bricks...

The "Toothache" sounds punishing...

Topsy-turvy; In a state of utter disorder or confusion.
Torment: Great physical pain or mental anguish.
Torpid: Deprived of the power of motion or feeling; benumbed; dormant.
Torpor: A condition of mental or physical inactivity or insensibility; apathy.
Torrid: Scorching; burning; dry; parched.

Are you getting a little "Touchy"?

Tramp: To wander about aimlessly; to trample.
Traitorous: Disloyal; faithless.
Trauma: A wound, especially one produced by sudden physical injury.
Travail: Strenuous mental or physical exertion; labor; toil.

Does He Make Our Punishments "Tremendous"?

****

You therefore must endure hardship as a good soldier of Jesus Christ.

2 TIMOTHY 2:3

WILLIAM E. BEAVERS

Treacherous: Betraying a trust; not to be relied upon.
Tremble: To feel or express fear or anxiety.
Trite: Overused and commonplace; lacking interest or originality; frayed.
Trivial: Of little important or significant; trifling; ordinary; commonplace.
Trollop: A slovenly, untidy woman; a loose woman; strumpet.
Tromp: To defeat soundly; trounce.
Tuckered: Weary, exhausted.
Tumble: To pitch headlong; stumble; fall.
Tuneless: Deficient in melody; unmusical.
Turgid: Over distended; swollen; bloated.
Turmoil: Utter confusion; extreme; agitation; tumult.
Tussle: To struggle; to scuffle.
Twaddle: Foolish, trivial, or idle talk or chatter.
Tweak: To pinch, pluck, or twist sharply.
Twinge: A sharp, sudden physical pain: A mental or emotional pain.
Tyke: A small mischievous child: A mean or uncouth fellow; boor.

"Try" not to sacrifice the life of your Child
because you can not find the "Time"!

****

**These shall be punished with everlasting destruction
from the presence of the Lord and from the glory
of His power, when He comes, in that Day,
to be glorified in His saints and to be admired
among all those who believe,
because our testimony among you was believed.**

2 THESSALONIANS 1:9-10

**Yes, and all who desire to live godly in Jesus
Christ will suffer persecution.
But evil men and imposters will grow worse and worse,
Deceiving and being deceived.
But you must continue in the things which you have learned
and be assured of, knowing from who you have learned *them,***

2 TIMOTHY 3:12-14

ALL ABOUT THE LETTER "T"

The "Teacher", "Technician" and the "Therapist" begin with the letter "T"
Do you lay "Tile" or work in the "Timber" Industry"?
Might you be in the "Trucking" business?

Whatever your chosen field I will venture to say it is rather "Tough"

"Take" the "Time" to "Teach" the Children...

"Try" harder...

"There" may be no "Tomorrow"

Quench your "Thirst" Reading the Bible...

"Thessalonians", "Timothy" and "Titus"

"Take" charge...

"Two-step" your way to Him...

Set the "Table" and serve up some "Tenderloins" and "Tomato"

Pay your "Taxes" no matter how "Tough" it seems...

Pass all HIS "Test"; "Trust" in Him and reign "Triumphant"
(The "Test", Trust" and "Triumphant" all begin and end with the letter "T")

Spend as much time getting to know the Lord as you do on the "Telephone!

"Turn" off the "Television" one night of the week and "Teach" them...

"Throw" a "Turkey" in the oven while you are at it...

The "Thousand Year Reign" awaits you...

THE "TIME" IS NOW!

THE END TIMES ARE HERE

By William Beavers

Evolution the Revolution and then all the Pollution'
What will be the Ultimate Solution?

The Resurrection of Jesus Christ' the second time' we have enticed.

Hear these words and quake with fear'
for the time draws quickly near!
Obsolete and Extinction Are punishments of His way.
The Poor and the humble for this day' they do pray,
Those that disbelieve, are you prepared to pay?
Jesus Christ is your savior' This the bible does say...
Without Him do you stand a chance' in this I say "nay"

So it seems the Book of Revelations is upon us,
What' you say is all the fuss?
Read about the hunger and the lust and how we shall return to dust!

As time draws near' shake with fear...
Hold those close to you' hold those that are so dear.
For the End times are here!

Find belief while there's still time
Give more than just one dime.
As time draws near,
Shiver with fear.

The glory belongs to Him' best learn to swim'
Hide if you can' for He is more than just a man!
On a pillar of clouds He will ride'
Watch as He rolls in with the Oceans great tide!

As time draws near
"Believe" and have nothing to fear
As time draws near.

It Has Begun...

318

HOW UNIQUE

UNEQUALED

Understanding...

U

Those things which are quite unique...

...Useless

*Understanding the letter "U" is somewhat complicated;
the definition itself represents: "**Uniqueness**"*

Without an "Understanding" we fall prey to "Useless"

*The capitol letter "U" sounds very similar to the word "You",
Might this give us some hint of the power of this letter?*

*Until we start to learn and to teach our children that "Ultimately"
it is the "Lord God" That is in full control, then our lives will /can
be controlled by the punishments of the Letters of the Alphabet...*

*Unless we wish upon our children all the "Ugliness" that the punishments can
bring, Might we instill upon them and ourselves the sacrifice of Jesus Christ!*

*Unconcerned...
Unbelievable...
Unacceptable...*

*Unfortunately there are many questions still "Unknown" about the complexity
of the Letters of our world and the part they do play; I will continue to learn...*

*"U" be the judge, will the Commonality of the letter "U"
give us those things in life, Which are quite "Unique"?*

Will You "Understand"?

**Take heed to yourself and to the doctrine.
Continue in them,
for in doing this you will save both
yourself and those that hear you.**

1 TIMOTHY 4:16

Do not forget the letter "U"

"U" are the key...

Notes

COMMONALITY OF THE LETTER "U"

Those things in life which are quite "Unique"

The "Udder" of the cow...

The "U-boat" and the "Ukulele"

The "Umbilical" cord...

The "Umbrella"

The "Umpire"

Your "Uncle"

"Uncle Sam"

"Underground"

The "Understudy" and the "Underwriter"

The "Undertaker"

"Unearthly"

The "Unicorn" and the "Unicycle"

"Unidentified Flying Objects"

The "Uniforms" we wear and the "Universal" joint...

The "Universe" and the "Universities"

"Unleaded" gas...

"Upholstery" "Uranium" "Urethane"

The "Urinal" and the "Urn"

Each of "Us"

The "United States of America"

The "Usher" and the State of "Utah"

"Utensils"

The "Uterus" and the "Uvula"

All the "Utilities"

****

For the law appoints as high priests men who have weakness, but the word of the oath, which came after the law, appoints the Son who has been perfected forever.

HEBREWS 7:28

The letter "U" sounds like "YOU"
Quite "Unique" and follows the "Q".
"Understanding" is what it takes'
Being "Useless" is for the fakes.
He's the one in "Ultimate" control...

When He returns, hide like a mole!

***

The letter "U" represents those things that are quite "Unique"
And the letter "N" represents those things that are "Needed"

As we "Unleash" the Rewards and Punishments
of the letter "U" keep this in Mind!

REWARDS OF THE LETTER "U"

Listening to the "Ukulele"

Ultimate:
Completing a series or process; final; conclusive.

"Ultra-"

An "Umbrella" when you need it...

The "UN-" rewards are next...

"Unadulterated" and "Unaffected" are a few...

Unalloyed:
Not in a mixture with other metals; pure.

"Unbending", "Unbroken", and "Unconditional" are a few more...

"Understanding" is the key...

..."Unequaled" is He!

"United" we stand...

One word "Under God"

Unity:
The state of being one; of agreement; unification.

Make it "Universal"

"Unlabored" and "Unlimited"

"Unlock" the door to His world...

"Unscathed" is His Reward...

"Unstressed" is Another...

"UN-wielding" is His Way!

Learn to "Unwind"

Look "Up" all those "Up-" words with someone you love...

Being "Upwind" might be a reward...

"Uplifting" sounds like Him...

"Upward" we will go...

The ability to "Urge" others...

Of the "Utmost" importance...

Knowing when not to "Utter" a word...

Take a "U-turn", save your soul and your loved ones...

****

**And with many other words he testified and exhorted them,
saying,
"Be saved from this perverse generation."
Then those who gladly received his word were baptized;
and that day about three thousand souls were added to *them*.
And they continued steadfastly in the
apostles' doctrine and fellowship,
in the breaking of bread, and in prayers.**

ACTS 2:40-42

The House of Jacob belongs to our Lord Jesus Christ...

***Are we Prepared for the Power of the "U"?
"Unfathomable" and "Unbeliever"
Will give you a Clue...***

WILLIAM E. BEAVERS

PUNISHMENTS OF THE LETTER "U"

Might the "U-boat" give us our punishment?

*Just plain "Ugly"
(A punishment passed down)?*

Have I given "U" an "Ulcer"?

Not having an "Umbrella" when you need it...

I will tell you for the "Umpteenth" time...

The "UN-" words are next...

*"Unaccomplished", "Unadvised", "Unappealing", "Unarmed", "Unattached"
"Unassisted", "Unaware", "Unbalanced", "Unbecoming", and "Unbelief"
"Unbuttoned", "Uncivil", "Unclean", "Unclear", and "Uncommitted"
"Unconscious", "Uncounted", "Unconsidered", "Uncouth"*

And six feet "Under"

"Undecided", Tell Me it isn't so...

*"Underbid", "Undercut", "Underfed", "Underpaid"
"Undeserving", "Undesirable", "Undirected"*

And your "Undoing"

"Unexpected", "Unfaithful", and "Unfit"

How "Unfortunate"

"Unfriendly", "Unfruitful", and "Ungainly"

Are you coming "Unglued"?

Say you're not "Ungodly"

That is very "Unhealthy"

"Unholy" leads to all the punishments...

"Unimproved", "Unkind", and being "Unknown" are a few more...

"Unlawful", "Unorganized", "Unpicked", "Unpleasant", and "Unpopular"

Do not be "Unprepared"

Are you becoming "Unraveled"?

Are you "Unready" for His return?

"Unrelenting" are the punishments of the "UN-"

"Unrighteous", "Unruly" and "Unsaved"
"Unskilled", "Unsociable", and "Unstable"
"Unsuspecting", "Unthankful", and "Unwise"

Do not be "Unworthy" of His sacrifice...

Will you be prepared for the "Uprising"?

There will be an "Uproar"

Have I "Upset" you?

He will not be "Upstaged"!

He can punish each of "Us"

He will punish the "USA"

Being rendered "Useless" is His way...

Utterly:
Complete: Absolutely; Entirely.

****

So they went out, they and all their armies with them,
***as* many people *as* the sand that *is* on the seashores in multitude,**
with very many horses and chariots.
And when all these kings had met together,
they came and camped together at the waters
of Merom to fight against Israel.

JOSHUA 11:4-5

ALL ABOUT THE LETTER "U"

The "Umpire", "Undertaker" and the
"Underwriter" begin with the letter "U"

Might you work at the local "University?

Whatever your chosen field I will venture to say it is quite "Unique"

Might "U" just be an "Underachiever"?

Are you still an "Unbeliever"?

"Uncover" the facts; learn the power of the Alphabet!

"Understanding" is the key...

"Ultimately" He is the one in control...

Learn to "Unwind"; rest for one day of the week...

Try riding a "Unicycle" or playing the "Ukulele"

"United" we stand...

"U" are important to Him...

"Use" your time to teach others...

"Unleash" the food, enjoy while "U" can...

Have you ever seen a "UFO"?

You might enjoy swimming?
(Underwater)

Try not to think about "U" so much...

"Unfortunately" as a Christian Nation we have failed.
Therefore His Wrath will Soon be "Upon" Us...

"Unless" We Can Change the Masses?

VICTORY

Vast

V

"Victorious" with Guidance...

Vague   Victim

Be "Very" Careful!

Victory belongs to Him...

Vast is His world...

Verify...

****

My son, if you receive my words,
And treasure my commands within you,
So that you incline your ear to wisdom,
And apply your heart to understanding;
Yes, if you cry out for discernment,
And lift up your voice for understanding,
If you seek her as silver,
And search for her as *for* hidden treasures;
Then you will understand the fear of the LORD,
And find the knowledge of God.
For the LORD gives wisdom;
From His mouth *comes* knowledge and understanding;
He stores up sound wisdom for the upright;
He is a shield to those who walk uprightly;
He guards the paths of justice,
And preserves the way of His saints.

PROVERBS 2:1-8

Verbal agreements are binding...

Visit Them in heaven...

Vanquish evil...

He guides us to "Victory" this the "V"
"Guidance Required" in our Dictionary you can see?
"Vast" is His domain, "Vulgarity" best try to refrain,
"Versatility" and "Vigor" yours when you jump on the train
In our "Vocabulary" More Punishments Remain.

COMMONALITY OF THE LETTER "V"

"Victorious with Guidance"

**All our common "V" words show to us that
with "Guidance", All lead to victory.**

"Verify" it on your own...

"Visibility" is for the believers...

"Veto" the unbelievers...

The "Verse" is next...

****

'Now if the whole congregation of Israel sins unintentionally,
and the thing is hidden from the eyes of the assembly,
and they have done *something against* any of
the commandments of the LORD
in anything which should not be done, and are guilty;
'when the sin which they have committed becomes known,
then the assembly shall offer a young bull for the sin,
and bring it before the tabernacle of meeting.

LEVITICUS 4:13-14

The "Vaccines" give us victory over the diseases...

The "Vacuum" gives us victory over the floors...

"Valet" parking...

"Validating" your work...

The "Valley" leads to many wonderful things...

The "Valve" stops the fluids from pouring out...

Being on the "Varsity" squad...

The "Varnish" protects the furniture...

331

The "Vase" displays the flowers...

The "Vasectomy"

"The "Vatican" needs guidance from the Lord...

The "Vault" will protect your valuables...

"Vegetables" lead us to a healthier life...

The "Vehicle" takes us where we need to go...
(How much guidance is required here)?

The "Veins" give victory to the heart....

The "Vent" and the "Ventilator"

All the "Verbs' give victory to our language...

The Bible "Verses"

Standing "Vertical"

The sailing "Vessel"

Victor:
One who defeats or vanquishes an adversary; the winner in a battle.

Victory:
Final and complete defeat of the enemy.

"Video" "Vines" "Vinyl" and the "Viola"

The "Virgin"

The "Visa" and the "Vise"

Our "Vision" and the "Visor"

Taking your "Vitamins"

Our "Vocabulary" will lead us to victory...

"Voice" your opinion...

The "Volcano" gives us new life; might it also be a punishment?

The "Volume" on the radio needs guidance...

"Vote" when you can...

All these things lead to "Victory" in one form or another.
All do need guidance from the heavens above...

Let Him Guide You...

****

And it will come to pass in that day
That the mountains shall drip with new wine,
The hills shall flow with milk,
And all the brooks of Judah shall be flooded with water;
A fountain shall flow from the house of the LORD
And water the valley of Acacias.

JOEL 3:18

The word "Government" starts with the letter "G"
Includes the letter "V" And ends with the letter "T"
The "President" begins with the "P" and ends with the "T"

(Triumphant or Tragedy)

(According to the Belief within)

Might things be a little "Vague" for you?

REWARDS OF THE LETTER "V"

Taking a "Vacation"

Having the "Vaccine" when you need it...

Being named "Valedictorian"

"Valentines" Day

Valiant:
Possessing or acting with valor: Brave; Courageous; Stouthearted.

Valor:
Courage and boldness, as in battle; Bravery

Being "Valuable" to Him...

Receiving a "Variety" of Rewards...

Being named to the "Varsity" Squad...
(Lead them Well)

Vast:
Very great in degree or intensity: Immense.

"Vaulting" ahead of others...

All the "Vegetables"

Venerable:
Worthy of reverence or respect by virtue of dignity and character.

Venturous:
Courageous and Daring: Adventurous and Bold.

Veracious:
Honest: Truthful and Accurate.

The ability to "Verify" the truth for ourselves is a nice way of rewarding us...

"Versatility" leads to many rewards...

As Does Reading the Bible "Verses"

****

So the multitude marveled when they saw *the* mute speaking, *the* maimed made whole, *the* lame walking, and *the* blind seeing; and they glorified the God of Israel.

MATTHEW 15:31

Vespers:
Any worship service held in the late afternoon or evening.

Our Father in Heaven and His Son, Our Savior Jesus Christ!
We pray this day that you will have Mercy on your Children,
For we are Blinded by Temptation and Deceived by Evil.
We lust for what others have and have not kept your Commandments.
From this day forward let "Righteousness" guide our every thought,
In this we pray.
AMEN

Anyway back to the Rewards...

Receiving good "Vibes"

Vibrant:
Pulsing or throbbing with energy or activity.

Being present at His "Victorious" "Victory"

Enjoy the "View"

You may want to start the "Vigil" now...

"Vigor" "Vintage" and being a "Virgin" are a few more...

Virility:
Masculine vigor: Manliness of thought or action.

Virtue:
The quality of moral excellence, righteousness, and responsibility.

"Visibility" is for the believers...

The "Vision" to understand the future...

It is "Vital"

He will make a "Vivid" Impression...

Understanding our "Vocabulary" will lead you to the ultimate Reward...

The ability to "Vocalize" our feelings...

Having Him "Vouch" for you...

Renewing your "Vows"

Enjoying the "Voyage"

****

After these things I looked, and behold,
a great multitude which no one could number,
of all nations, tribes, peoples, and tongues,
standing before the throne and before the Lamb,
clothed with white robes, with palm branches in their hands,
and crying out with a loud voice, saying,
"Salvation *belongs* to our God who sits
on the throne, and to the Lamb!"

REVELATION 7:9-10

Then one of the elders answered, saying to me,
"Who are these arrayed in white robes,
and where did they come from?"
And I said to him,
"Sir, you know."
So he said to me,
"These are the ones who come out of the great tribulation,
and washed their robes and made them
white in the blood of the Lamb.

REVELATION 7:13-14

- THE RAPTURE -

PUNISHMENTS OF THE LETTER "V"

Vacant:
Containing nothing: Empty; unfilled.

Not having the "Vaccine" when you need it...

Vagabond/Vagrant:
An itinerant beggar or thief: Aimless; unstable.

Might things seem a little "Vague" for you?

Try not to be so "Vain"

Vampire:
A woman who uses sexual attraction to exploit men.

"Vandalized" in your own home...

Or will you simply "Vanish"?

"Vaporized"

Is this all to "Vast" for you?

Turned into a "Vegetable"

Receiving all His "Vengeance"

Vexed:
To irritate or annoy, as with petty importunities: Bother; pester.

Getting the bad "Vibes"

Vicious:
Behaving in an unruly or potentially dangerous manner.

Becoming the next "Victim"

Vile:
Miserably poor: wretched; depraved; loathsome.

Vindictive:
Unforgiving: Bitter; Spiteful.

Having to Deal with all the "Violence" Is a form of Punishment for us All...

Being "Violated" is another...

Catching a "Virus", Stuck in the "Vise"

And a "Visitor" from below...

Null and "Void"

Volatile:
Tending to violence: Explosive.

"Volcanoes"

Do you feel like "Vomiting" yet?

Placed under a "Voodoo" spell...

Being a "Voyeur"

Refrain from all the "Vulgarity"

Being "Vulnerable"

Eaten by "Vultures"

****

So I looked,
and behold,
a pale horse.
And the name of him who sat on it was Death,
and Hades followed with him.
And power was given to them over a fourth of the earth,
to kill with sword,
with hunger,
with death,
and by the beasts of the earth.

REVELATION 6:8

ALL ABOUT THE LETTER "V"

The "Veterinarian", "Video-Repairman" and the "Valet-Driver"

Might you be A "Vice-President"?

Eat Your "Vegetables" and try some "Veal"

Do you drive a "Van"?
How many "Vehicles" do you own?

Might you have lots of "Varicose Veins"?

You are "Valuable"

Do you like the "Vermouth"?

Add some "Vanilla"

Take a "Vacation" go "Visit" the "Vatican"

Try playing "Volleyball"

Are you a "Veteran"?

"Voice" your opinion...

The "Verse" is next...

****

"Here *is* the mind which has wisdom:
The seven heads are seven mountains
on which the woman sits.
"There are also seven kings.
Five have fallen, one is, *and* the other has not yet come.
And when he comes, he must continue a short time.
"The beast that was,
and is not,
is himself also the eighth,
and is of the seven,
and is going to perdition.

REVELATION 17:9-11

Notes

WOW

Wonderful   Women

(Similar to the letter "M", lots of ups and downs, more ups however)

Makes a "Vivid Impression"

Our Lord God says WOW…

Wants   Worry   Wishes

Wacky   Weird

Living on the "Wild" side…

Which path Will you follo$W$...

Waiting is Wrong...

Why?

What is the Worst that can happen?

Where will it lead you?

Will you be ready?

Worry...

****

Therefore strengthen the hands which hang down,
and the feeble knees,
and make straight paths for your feet,
so that what is lame may not be dislocated,
but rather be healed.
Pursue peace with all *people,*
and holiness,
without which no one will see the Lord:

Hebrews 12:12-14

But do not forget to do good and to share,
for with such sacrifices God is well pleased.

Hebrews 13:16

COMMONALITY OF THE LETTER "W"

Our Lord God says "WOW"

*Might the letter "W" give us all those things that
make a "vivid impression" on us also?*

Our "Wages" and the "Wager" you just placed...

The "Wagon" and your "Waistline"

The "Wake" for the deceased...

The "Walls" and the "Wallet"

The "Walrus" and the "Walleye"

The "Waiter" and the "Waltz"

"War"

The "Warden" and your "Wardrobe"

The "Warehouse" and the "Warranty"

The "Wash-cloth", "Washer" and even the "Wasp"

The "Waste" and all the "Water"

"Watercolors" and those things that are "Waterproof"

*The "Waterslide" and the "Water-ski"
(Enjoy this life)*

The "Waves" also make a vivid impression on Him...

"Wax", "Wealth", "Weapons", and the things we "Wear"

How about the "Weather" and the spider "Web"

He says wow when we "Wed" and to all the "Weeds"

He says wow to Each "Week" that passes by...

He says "Wow" to the "Weekend" and to our "Weight"

He says "Wow" to the "Well" you just dug, and to the entire "West"

343

"West-point" and the "Whale"

The "Wharf" and the "Wheat"

The "Wheel" and the "Whip"

The "Whirlpool" and the "Whirlwind"

The "Whistle" and all the "White"

"The "Widow" and the "Wife"

The "Wilderness" and the "Wildfire"

"The "Willow" tree and the "Wind"

The "Windmill" and the "Window"

The "Wine" and the "Wings" of the bird...

The "Winter" most definitely makes a vivid impression...

The "Witch" the "Witness" and the "Wizard"

"The "Wolf" and the "Woman"

"Wood" and the "Wool"

All the "Words"

He says "Wow" to the Whole "World"!

****

**Blessed *is* he who reads and those who
hear the words of this prophecy,
and keep those things which are written in it;
for the time *is* near.**

REVELATION 1:3

REWARDS OF THE LETTER "W"

A "Wad" of cash...

A vanilla "Wafer"

An honest "Wage"

A nice "Waist-line"

"Waking" with the Lord...

A "Waldorf" Salad...

Taking a nice "Walk"

Catching a "Walleye"

"Walnuts" and doing the "Waltz"

A Magic "Wand"

"Wanting" nothing more...

Being nice and "Warm"

The ability to "Warn" others...

"Warp" speed...

Having enough "Water"

Owning "Waterfront" property...

A slice of "Watermelon"

Wealth:
A great quantity of valuable material possessions or resources:
Riches; Well being.

Might the "Wedding" be a reward?

Enjoying the "Weekend"

"Welcoming" others get you His Rewards...

All those words that begin with the word "Well-"

345

Seeing a "Whale"

Knowing "Which" path to choose...

Whimsical:
Capricious: Playful; Fantastic.

The ability to "Whistle" while you work...

Getting the "Whole" Picture...

Buying "Wholesale"

Wholesome:
Conductive to sound health or well-being.

A taste of the "Wild" side...

The entire "Wilderness"

Having a legal "Will"

"Willing" to accept the inevitable...

Win:
To achieve success in an effort or venture: Achieving victory.

Windfall:
A sudden and unexpected piece of good fortune.

A nice glass of "Wine"

A "Winning" personality...

Wisdom:
Understanding of what is true, right, or lasting.

Having all your "Wishes" granted sounds like a nice Reward...

Wit:
The natural ability to perceive or know:
Understanding; Intelligence; good sense.

Witty:
Possessing or demonstrating wit in speech or writing:
Clever and humorous.

Might "Woman" be a Reward for all Mankind?
Or might it be a Punishment?
(Trying to be "witty" here)

Being considered "Wonderful" sounds like a nice Reward.

The ability to "Woo" others...

Understanding all the "Words"

"Working" when you want to...

Might the whole "World" be a form of His reward to us?

The ability to know who to "Worship"

Worthy:
Having worth, merit, or value; useful or admirable.

The ability to "Write" for the Lord has been My most fulfilling Reward!

****

**And everyone who has left houses
or brothers or sisters or father
or mother or wife or children or lands,
for my sake,
shall receive a hundredfold,
and inherit eternal life.**

MATTHEW 19:29

PUNISHMENTS OF THE LETTER "W"

Wacky:
Highly irrational or erratic: Crazy; Silly

Wail:
To grieve or protest audibly, suggestive of a cry.

"Waiting" in line...

"Wait" and see...

"Walking" aimlessly...

Dealing with the "Walk-out"

"Walking" over others will lead to Many Punishments...

An Empty "Wallet"

Getting "Walloped"

Walloped:
To beat soundly: To strike with a hard blow.

"Wallowing" in your own sorrows...

Wander:
To move about with no destination or purpose.

"Wanting" More...

"War"

A visit to the psychiatric "Ward"

Not understanding the "Warning"

A "Warrant" for your arrest...

"Warts"

"Wasted" and "Wasteful"

Slammed by a "Wave" is a small Reminder of His punishments.

"Wave" goodbye...

"Weak", "Weary", and just plain "Weird"

"Whacked" by the rod...

Whine:
To utter a plaintive, high-pitched sound, as in pain, fear, or complaint.

Lashed by the "Whip" or just an out and out "Whipping"

Just plain "Wicked"

Having a "Wife"
(Smile)

Unable to "Wiggle" your way out of a mess...

Lost in the "Wilderness"

Struck by a "Wild" pitch...

A lack of "Willpower"

"Wilting" away...

A victim of a "Witch-hunt"

Withdrawn:
Not readily approached: Isolated; Modest

"Without"

Not having a "Witness" when you need it...

Woeful:
Mournful, pitiful, or deplorable.

Are you feeling "Woozy" yet?

Many are the Punishments of our Ways!

Worn:
Affected by wear or use; Impaired or damaged.

"Worry"

Getting "Worse"

And being the "Worst"

"Worthless", "Wounded", and "Wracked" by pain...

Wrathful:
Full of wrath; fiercely angry.
(Are we prepared for His)?

Wreak:
To inflict vengeance or punishment.

Are you a "Wreck" about now?

Wretched:
Living in degradation and misery; miserable.

"Wrinkled" like a prune...

Always being "Wrong"

"Wrung" out to dry...

****

Then the sky receded as a scroll when it is rolled up and every mountain and island was moved out of its place.

REVELATION 6:14

ALL ABOUT THE LETTER "W"

The "Writer", "Weatherman" and the "Waiter"

Might you work on "Wall-Street"?

"Will" you be ready?

"Wait" and see...

"Wish"

Take up "Whittling"

One word "Women"
Or might it be "Watermelon"?

Might you go through lots of ups and downs in your life?

Do you enjoy "Wrestling" with the kids?

All "Work" and no play is not healthy.
(Rest One Day)

Have a glass of "Wine"
(Know your limits)

Do you wear a "Watch"?

"Waste" not, "Want" not

"Worship" Him...

Sometimes you are "Wrong"
Sometimes you are Right...

"Where" "O" "Where" have you gone?

***

In the beginning was the Word,
and the Word was with God,
and the Word was God.

JOHN 1:1

Notes

"X" MARKS THE SPOT

X

Exactly how things Are/will be...
(Exception to the rule)

X-Ray It...

E**X**perience His Power...

E**X**plain it to Others...

****

But the children of Israel were fruitful and increased abundantly,
multiplied and grew exceedingly mighty;
and the land was filled with them.
Now there arose a new king over Egypt,
who did not know Joseph.
And he said to his people,
Look,
the people of the children of Israel *are* more and mightier than we;
"come let us deal shrewdly with them,
lest they multiply,
and it happen,
in the event of war,
that they also join our enemies and fight against us,
and so go up out of the land."

Exodus 1:7-10

*****

Guess what letter we see next, you got it right the letter "X"
"Exception" to the rule' with this letter He did fool.
Drop the silent "E", then might you see what will come to be?
"Examine" it thoroughly' the "Extraterrestrial" could we see,
"Exact", "Extreme" and "Exceptionally"
Are words that fit this category!

COMMONALITY OF THE LETTER "X"

"X" MARKS THE SPOT!

The letter "X' shows us "Exactly" how it is/will be...

"Exception" to the Rule...

Check out all the "EX" words too...

Just drop the Silent "E"

"Examine" those words in the Dictionary...

"Extraterrestrial" fits into this category...

"Extreme"

"Exactly"

"Execute" your Authority...

****

So the LORD said to him,
"Who has made man's mouth?
Or who makes the mute, the deaf, the seeing, or the blind?
Have not I, the Lord?
"Now therefore,
go,
and I will be with your mouth and
teach you what you shall say."

EXODUS 4:11

"Experience" Him for Yourself...

The letter "X" is the Symbol for Christianity!

("X" Marks the Spot)

It also represents "CHRIST"

XP:
A Monogram used to represent Christ or Christianity;
Composed of chi *and* rho,
The first two letters of the Greek word for Christ...

Might we "Expect" His return soon?

Will it be "X-Rated?

The "Xerox" Machine makes an "Exact" copy...

The "X-Ray" Machine shows us "Exactly" what we need to see...

The "EX" words are next...

Exact/Exactly:
Accurate and precise: Strictly and completely in accord with fact.

Examine:
To Inspect or Scrutinize in Detail; Observe or Analyze Carefully.

If we make an "Example" of Someone or Something,
Does This show us what to "Expect"?

Excavate:
To "Expose" or uncover by digging.

The "Exclamation" point...

We can "Expect" the "Excrement"

The "Excuses" too...

The "Execution" seems pretty "Exact"?

The "Executive" gets the "Exact" orders from the Big Man.

(Might This Be An Executive Order)?

Exemplar:
One that is Worthy of being copied: A Model.

The "Exhibit" gives us a clue...

"Existence" is what it is all about...

The "Exit" shows us "Exactly" where to go...

"Expand" the word...

"Expect" the Unexpected...

"Expectant" shows us the baby is on the way...

Expedite:
To Issue Officially.

"Experience" tells us "Exactly" what to "Expect" next...

...As does the "Experiment"

The "Explanation" is in the reading...

How "Explicit" Does He need to make it?

Will it take an "Explosion" to show us?

"Explore" the Dictionary, Read what You Understand?

Expound:
To give a detailed statement of: To set forth.

The "Extraterrestrial" could we see next?

**

Two bright stars in the glorious night sky
A twist and a turn from not one but two
Out of sight in the blink of an eye' they did fly
Extraterrestrials' what should I do?
No one would believe' not even you!

REWARDS OF THE LETTER "X"

"Xmas"

Listening to the "Xylophone"

Knowing "Exactly" what to expect...

Exalted:
Elevated in rank, character, position, or the like.

Leading by "Example"

"Exceeding" His expectations...

Excel:
To be better than; surpass; outdo.

Excellence/Excellent:
Being of the highest or finest quality; superb.

"Exceptional" are the rewards...

The ability to "Excite" others...

Being an "Exclusive" member of His team...

Exempt:
To free from an obligation or duty required of others.

"Exhilaration" and the ability to "Exhort" the message...

Might our very "Existence" be a form of reward?

Exonerate:
To free from a charge; declare blameless.

Exotic:
Strikingly and intriguingly unusual or beautiful.

The ability to "Expand" our beliefs...

"Expecting" the unexpected...

Being an "Expectant" mother is a nice reward,
However now is not the time...

Guiding others through "Experience"

Being an "Expert" about it...

Expertise:
Specialized knowledge.

The ability to "Explain" it thoroughly...

"Explicit" enough?

"Exploring" the unknown...

"Expressing" His wishes...

He is "Exquisite"

Receiving an "Extension" of His world...

Getting "Extra"

How "Extraordinary"

Exuberant:
Full of high spirits; abundantly joyous.

Exult:
To rejoice greatly; be jubilant or triumphant.

****

Then Moses answered and said,
But suppose they will not believe me or listen to my voice;
suppose they say,
"The LORD has not appeared to you."

EXODUS 4:1

Will You Believe?

PUNISHMENTS OF THE LETTER "X'

The "Ex" wife/husband (Smile)

Exaggerated:
Unduly emphasized or magnified; going beyond truth or fact.

Exasperate:
To make very angry or irritated.

Being made an "Example" of...

"Excise" tax...

"Excluded" from entering Heaven...

All the "Excuses"

Being "Executed"

Unable to "Exhale", "Exhaustion" and "Exiled"

Unable to find the "Exit"

"Expelled"

"Expensive" and "Expired"

Ready to "Explode"

"Exploited" and "Exposed"

Expunge:
To omit, erase, strike out, or obliterate.

"EXTINCTION"

****

The letter "X" is a very "Exact"
Description of the things that await those who are not prepared.
I write this not to scare you, but to warn you.

ALL ABOUT THE LETTER "X"

"Except" the responsibility...

"Examine" the book of Revelations...

Get "Excited"

"TeXas"

"MeXico"

Let us not forget the "Extraterrestrial"

"Explore" the possibilities...

"X-ray" the dictionary...

"Excuses" are easy to come by...

Do you always miss the "Exit" ramp?

"Experience" goes a long way...

"Experience" Them...

Are you always the "Expert"?

"Explain" it to others...

****

**Then the temple of God was opened in heaven,
and the ark of His covenant was seen in His temple.
And there were lightings, noises, thunderings,
an earthquake, and great hail.**

REVELATION 11:19

Notes

THE FOUNTAIN OF YOUTH

YOUTHFUL   YOUNG

The Fountain of Youth...
(Caution needed)

Yesterday

"You" are the key...

*"**You**" starts with the letter "Y":*
Will this letter have a tendency to make us think more About Ourselves?
The answer is "Yes"!

"Yearning" for more...

You might also look up the letter "U"

Slowing down a little in life is all that is required;
The Lord God teaches "You" this...

Might the Capitol letter "Y" be the true "Fountain of Youth"
That Mankind has Been Searching for since the Beginning of Time?
(The answer is "Yes")

Use "Your" God Given abilities...

Yell it out...

****

"Whenever I have moved about with all the children of Israel,
have I ever spoken a word to anyone from the tribes of Israel,
whom I command to shepherd My people Israel,
saying,
'Why have you not built Me a house of cedar?' '"
"Now therefore, thus shall you say to My servant David,
'Thus says the LORD of hosts:
"I took you from the sheepfold, from following the sheep,
to be ruler over My people, over Israel.
"And I have been with you wherever you have gone,
and have cut off all your enemies from before you,
and have made you a great name,
like the name of the great men who *are* on the earth.
"Moreover I will appoint a place for My people Israel,
and will plant them,
that they may dwell in a place of their own and move no more:
nor shall the sons of wickedness oppress them anymore,
as previously,
"since the time that I commanded judges
to be over My people Israel,
and have caused you to rest from all your enemies.
Also the LORD tells you that He will make you a house."

2 SAMUEL 7:7-11

COMMONALITY OF THE LETTER "Y"

**"Young" at heart, slow to mature and even
looking "Youthful" longer!**

***

"Yesterday" takes us back in time...

The "Yield Sign" and the "Yellow light" slow our progress...

*How slowly does the "Year" go by?
Might the older we get the quicker it seem?*

*Yarn:
A long, complicated story or tale of real or fictitious adventures
often elaborated upon by the teller during the telling.*

Yen: A "yearning" a longing for.

*Young/Youth:
The Vigor or enthusiasm or other characteristics of this period.*

Yore: Time long past.

Yet: At some future time, eventually.

Looking at your old "Yearbook" will take you back in time...

Trying out "Yoga" might just help "You" to cope with life...

*"Your" belief in the Lord God and the sacrifice that Jesus Christ
made is what will help You refrain from all the "Yelling"*

****

**"Thus speaks the LORD GOD of Israel,
Saying:
"Write in a book for yourself all the
words that I have spoken to you.**

JERIMIAH 30:2

REWARDS OF THE LETTER "Y"

Yahweh:
A name for God assumed by modern scholars...

Might having the nice "Yard" to frolic in be a reward?

Yare:
Responding easily; manageable; bright; lively; quick; ready.

The ability to say "Yes" when asked of something sounds like a nice reward...

Yearn:
To feel deep pity, sympathy, or tenderness.

Yippee:
Used to express joy or elation.

The "Yogurt" in the refrigerator sounds good...

Staying "Young" longer seems to be what all of us are after?

Youthful: Possessing youth; still young; fresh; active.
Yule: Christmas or the season or feast celebrating Christmas.
Yummy: Delightful; delicious.

What More Could "You" ask for?

****

For you are all sons of God through faith in Christ Jesus.
For as many of you as were baptized into Christ have put on Christ.
There is neither Jew nor Greek, there is neither slave nor free,
there is neither male nor female;
for you are all one in Christ Jesus.
And if you are Christ's,
then you are Abraham's seed,
and heirs according to the promise.

GALATIANS 3:26-29

PUNISHMENTS OF THE LETTER "Y"

Yak:
To talk or chatter persistently and meaninglessly.

Yammer:
To complain peevishly or whisperingly; to whine.

Yanked:
To pull or extract suddenly; to jerk.

Yap:
To bark sharply or shrilly; yelp; to talk noisily or stupidly; jabber.

Might taking care of the "Yard" be a chore for you?

Yawn:
To open the mouth wide with a deep inspiration, usually involuntary, from drowsiness, fatigue, or boredom.

Yell/Yelp:
To cry out loudly, as in pain, fright: shouting.

Yowl:
To utter a loud, long, mournful cry; to howl; wail.

Is it possible that because the Lord God looks favorably upon the "young" That there are few punishments?

Remember "You" are the letter "U" also...

"You" are the Key to our Lord God, Set a good example for others...

What gives "You" the Right to Change the Rules of the Lord God?

Ask "Yourself" if those family and friends that you know that have the letter "Y" in their Names fit into this category?

****

**Therefore the sin of the young men was
very great before the LORD,
for men abhorred the offering of the LORD.**

1 SAMUEL 2:17

ALL ABOUT THE LETTER "Y"

"You" will do whatever work "You" choose...

Try not to think only of "Yourself"

Might your favorite color be "Yellow"?

"Yogurt" and "Yams"

Do you own a "Yacht"?

Say you're not a "Yankees" fan...

Try to refrain from all the "Yelling"

The "Ying" and the "Yang", might you yearn for a partner?

You Are Quite "Unique"

Do "You" Remember the punishments of the letter "U"?

"Understanding" is what it is all about...

Will "You" know what to do?

****

**They sing the song of Moses,
the servant of God,
and the song of the Lamb,
saying:
"Great and marvelous *are* Your works,
Lord God Almighty!
Just and true *are* Your ways,
O King of the saints!
Who shall not fear You,
O Lord, and glorify Your name?
For *You* alone *are* holy.
For all nations shall come and worship before You,
For Your judgments have been manifested."**

REVELATION 15:3-4

Notes

ZEALOUS

Z

(Similar to the letter "I" and the letter "S")

A little laid back...

Z Z Z "S

(Time for a nap)

371

WILLIAM E. BEAVERS

Might those with the letter "Z" also deal with the letters "I" and "S"?
A little more laid back however...

Zip to Him...

Zap the enemy...

****

So the angel who spoke with me said to me,
"Proclaim, saying, 'Thus says the LORD of hosts:
"I am zealous for Jerusalem
And for Zion with great zeal.
I am exceedingly angry with the nations at ease;
For I was a little angry,
And they helped-*but* with evil *intent*."
"Therefore thus says the LORD:
"I am returning to Jerusalem with mercy;
My house shall be built in it," says the LORD of hosts,
"And a *surveyor's* line shall be stretched out over Jerusalem.'"
"Again proclaim, saying,
"Thus says the LORD of hosts:
"My cities shall again spread out through prosperity;
The LORD will again comfort Zion,
And will again choose Jerusalem.'" "

ZECHARIAH 1:14-17

Do Not Sleep through it...

Can we Delay the In-evitable If He has already started the process?

LORD we pray for forgiveness...

372

COMMONALITY OF THE LETTER "Z"

A little bit laid back...

The "Zebra" has been chilling for a long time...

Zephyr:
A gentle wind.

Adding the number "Zero" to any other number
still gets you the same number...

Visiting the "Zoo" gives us a day to unwind...

The "ZZZ's" send us to sleep...

How many other "Z" words do you know?

You Might want to look up all those words in our
Vocabulary that include the letter "Z"

"Pizza", " Drizzle" and "Lazy" are a few...

****

Be silent in the presence of the Lord GOD:
For the day of the LORD *is* at hand,
For the LORD has prepared a sacrifice;
He has invited His guests.

ZEPHANIAH 1:7

***

"I will bring distress upon men,
And they shall walk like blind men,
Because they have sinned against the LORD;
Their blood shall be poured out like dust,
And their flesh like refuse."
Neither their silver nor gold
Shall be able to deliver them
In the day of the LORD'S wrath;
But the whole land shall be devoured
By the fire of His jealousy,
For He will make speedy riddance
Of all those who dwell in the land.

ZEPHANIAH 1:17-18

Gather yourselves together, yes, gather together,
O undesirable nation,
Before the decree is issued,
Or the day passes like chaff,
Before the LORD'S fierce anger comes upon you,
Before the day of the LORD'S anger comes upon you!
Seek the LORD, all you meek of the earth,
Who have upheld His justice.
Seek righteousness, seek humility.
It may be that you will be hidden
In the day of the LORD'S anger.

ZEPHANIAH 2:1-3

REWARDS OF THE LETTER "Z"

Zeal:
Enthusiastic and diligent devotion in pursuit of a cause, idea, or goal.

Zest:
Spirited enjoyment; wholehearted interest; gusto.

The ability to "Zip" into action...

Zippy:
Full of energy; brisk; lively; snappy.

Being in the "Zone"

A visit to the "Zoo"

"Zooming" to Him...

Your Rewards are also listed under the letters "I" and "S"

****

PUNISHMENTS OF THE LETTER "Z"

Zany:
A ludicrous, buffoonish character; given to outlandish behavior.

"Zapped" by the Rod...

Having to be told for the "Zillionth" time...

Becoming a "Zombie"

Zonked:
Intoxicated by alcohol or narcotics.

Many more Punishments remain under the "I' and "S' letters.

****

I will leave in your mist
A meek and humble people,
And they shall trust in the name of the LORD.
The remnant of Israel shall do no unrighteousness
And speak no lies,
Nor shall deceitful tongue be found in their mouth;
For they shall feed *their* flocks and lie down,
And no one shall make *them* afraid."

ZEPHANIAH 3:12-13

*****

"For then I will restore to the peoples a pure language,
That they all may call on the name of the LORD,
To serve Him with one accord.

ZEPHANIAH 3:9

ALL ABOUT THE LETTER "Z"

You can move quickly if you want to...

You are kin to the letter "S"

"Zucchini"

The Xylophone sounds like it starts with the letter "Z"

The Word "Lazy" sounds like it ends with the letter "Z"

Do not forget the Pizza...

Try a visit to "Zion" National Park...

You might want to stay,
Or are you just along for the ride?

****

And it shall come to pass in all the land,
Says the LORD,
"*That* two-thirds in it shall be cut off *and* die,
But *one*-third shall be left in it;
I will bring the *one*-third through the fire,
Will refine them as silver is refined,
And test them as gold is tested.
They will call on My name,
And I will answer them.
I will say,
"This *is* My people';
And each one will say,
"The LORD *is* my God.'"

ZECHARIAH 13:8-9

****

"But none of these things move me;
nor do I count my life dear to myself,
so that I may finish my race with joy,
and the ministry which I received from the Lord Jesus,
to testify to the gospel of the grace of God.
"And indeed,
now I know that you all,
among whom I have gone preaching the kingdom of God,
will testify to you this day that *I am*
innocent of the blood of all *men*.
"For I have not shunned to declare to
you the whole counsel of God.
"Therefore take heed to yourselves and to all the flock,
among which the Holy Spirit has made you overseers,
to shepherd the church of God which
He purchased with His own blood.
"For I know this,
that after my departure savage wolves
will come in among you,
not sparing the flock.
"Also from among yourselves men will rise up,
speaking perverse things,
to draw away the disciples after themselves.
"Therefore watch,
and remember that for three years
I did not cease to warn everyone night and day with tears.
"So now, brethren,
I command you to God and to the word of His grace,
which is able to build you up
and give you an inheritance among
all those who are sanctified.

ACTS 20:24-32

****

Then I, John, saw the holy city,
New Jerusalem,
coming down out of heaven from God,
prepared as a bride adorned for her husband.
And I heard a loud voice from heaven saying,
"Behold, the tabernacle of God *is* with men,
and He will dwell with them,
and they shall be His people.
God Himself will be with them *and be* their God.
"And God will wipe away every tear from their eyes;
there shall be no more death,
nor sorrow, nor crying.
There shall be no more pain,
for the former things have passed away."
Then He who sat on the throne said,
"Behold, I make all things new."
And He said to me,
Write, for these words are true and faithful."
And He said to me, "It is done!
I am the Alpha and the Omega,
the Beginning and the End.
I will give of the fountain of the water
of life freely to him who thirsts.
"He who overcomes shall inherit all things,
and I will be his God and he shall be My son.

REVELATION 21:2-7

****

"Lord, now You are letting Your servant depart in peace,
According to Your word;
For my eyes have seen Your salvation
Which You have prepared before the face of all peoples,
A light to bring revelation to the Gentiles,
And the glory of Your people Israel."

LUKE 2:29-32

****

See with what large letters I have written to you with my own hand!

GALATIANS 6:11

THE END?

***

Forty years in the wilderness is what it took'
To Enlighten Me to His special book
The mid-life crisis is what They say' take it as you may
A trip to Heaven this I pray.

Lust and Sin this for many Men!
Follow not One but Ten'
The Commandments is where it shall begin...
Teach others of the sacrifice'
Or take Your Chance and roll the dice
Preach the Word' to Others Entice.

Teach Others of His love' teach others of His Word'
For He sees through the Eyes of many a Bird
I have seen His image' I have Heard...
Disbelief in me' How Absurd!

How Mighty are His ways that through Clouds' He Designs
How Mighty are His signs that evil soon Resigns!

Forty Years in the Wilderness is what it Took'
To Enlighten Me to His Special Book

A True Believer Now' Wow!

***

**And I thank Christ Jesus our Lord who has enabled me,
because He counted me faithful,
putting *me* into the ministry,
although I was formerly a blasphemer,
a persecutor and an insolent man;
but I obtained mercy because I did *it* ignorantly in unbelief.**

1 TIMOTHY 1:12-13

CONCLUSION

The Capitol letter "A"
"I am the "Alpha" and the Omega"
New, First, Beginning, Start of...

The Capitol letter "B"
Watched more closely, seen more clearly...
Beware He Sees all...

The Capitol letter "C"
Lacks "true" Conviction...
(It can be achieved; Jesus Christ is our example)

The Capitol Letter "D"
Strength in the "D", good and evil...

The Capitol Letter "E"
"EARTHLY"

The Capitol Letter "F"
All our /His "Favorite things...

The Capitol Letter "G"
The Life and Times of the Lord God...

The Capitol Letter "H"
Heaven or Hell, either/or? Both...

The Capitol Letter "I"
The Invasion or Incapable of...

The Capitol Letter "J"
The Life and Times of our Savior Jesus Christ...

The Capitol Letter "K"
"Deceitful"

The Capitol Letter "L"
Life made easier, tough at the beginning...

The Capitol Letter "M"
Mans World, lots of ups and downs...

The Capitol Letter "N"
Needed but has Needs...

The Capitol Letter "O"
Completes life, especially for others...

The Capitol Letter "P"
A more "Profound Purpose"

The Capitol Letter "Q"
A Thorn in the side...

The Capitol Letter "R"
Life Exemplified; guidance required

The Capitol Letter "S"
The Traveler in mind/body/soul...

The Capitol Letter "T"
Tribulation, tough times, tests...

The Capitol Letter "U"
Those things which are quite unique...

The Capitol Letter "V"
"Victorious" with Guidance...

The Capitol Letter "W"
Makes a "Vivid Impression"

The Capitol Letter "X"
Exactly how things Are/will be...

The Capitol Letter "Y"
The Fountain of Youth...

The Capitol Letter "Z"
A little laid back...

A Little about the "Double Letter Syndrome"

*Each and every word in our vocabulary that includes two of the same letters
Side by side will show us the "Struggle within".*

*Every common word in our language with two of the same letters side
by side will show to us that there is a struggle with its true definition.*

The exception to the rule is the letter "T"; this one becomes much tougher!

*Might this show to us that those who have two of the same letters side by
side in their "God-given" names face additional struggles in this life?*

*Might there be a few of our letters that actually
become a little better when doubled?*

Might we learn from this and Name "His" Children a little differently?

Can having more letters in our name give us more knowledge?

Or might it give us more Rewards and Punishments to deal with?

Might it be more difficult to find a soul mate for those with long first names?

There is much to learn...

The time I could spend with the letters will last me a lifetime,

However short it might be...

I Am truly fascinated each and every day that He teaches.

*Our "God-Given" Names and the "faith" we carry within Ourselves
Is what sets Each of us apart.*

*Our Initials are Key in that they are Capitol letters.
Multiple letters that do not lie side by side follow in subsequent order.
(This has the tendency to strengthen the letter)*

The individual letters are next.
(And remember that those with letters that sound like
others can receive all that each give to them).

ALL the letters do come with good and evil...

How strong is the "Double Letter Syndrome"?

More studies can be made...

****

Who do you say that I Am?

Am I the seed of Abraham?
A Great, Great, Great, etc., etc., etc., Grandson...

Or the Spirit of Elijah?

Might I have had a Revelation from Jesus Christ?

Might it be All?

I am the Irish/Indian, the tribes of Judah and Levi?
(Remember page 176)

It is all here for us in black and white,
Will we choose to deny it because we cannot accept it?
Will the truth be too much for you to handle?
Will you simply choose to be raptured?

OR

Does the 1000Year Reign Await You?

THE CONQUERER:

**And I saw, and behold a white horse: and
he that sat on him had a bow;
And a crown was given unto him: and he went
forth conquering, And to conquer.**

(REVELATIONS 6:2)

**Can a book be a conqueror?
How many billions of souls has the Bible Conquered?**

**The white horse represents purity, truth,
righteousness (The Word of GOD)
Written by a Sagittarian (thus the bow)
Who received a revelation from Jesus Christ (thus the crown)
And the rest is history....**

**Many scholars and theologians have debated this subject often.
Some believe it is an antichrist of sorts.
Others believe it is the Word of God!
What do you now believe?**

You have been warned...

AUTHOR BIOGRAPHY

William Beavers understands the importance of the English Alphabet and how God uses it through our individual names to give to each of us our own traits, punishments, and rewards. After having received a personal revelation, he began writing this book so that other Christians might also be touched by the powers of the English alphabet and to relay a message he received. He currently resides in Oklahoma City, Oklahoma, and has two grown children. He spends most of his time teaching all those who are willing to listen, the importance of faith and knowledge.

"And the Jews marveled and said; how does this man know letters having never studied …" (John 7:15 NKJV)

SPECIAL THANKS TO WESTBOW PRESS

COMMENTS AND/OR DONATIONS MAY BE MADE TO:

THE CHURCH *of* ALPHATOLOGY

2119 Riverwalk Drive
Number 193
Moore, OK 73160

THE AUTHORS E-MAIL ADDRESS IS:

alphatology@yahoo.com

CPSIA information can be obtained
at www.ICGtesting.com
Printed in the USA
BVHW040817130520
579599BV00008B/158